CW01475809

DADS-TO-BE: FIRST-TIME FATHERS GUIDE

USE POWERFUL SKILLS TO BUILD CONFIDENCE, STRENGTHEN YOUR RELATIONSHIP, AND MASTER FATHERHOOD FOR A HEALTHY WORK FAMILY BALANCE

D. MOSON

© **Copyright 2024 D. MoSon. All rights reserved.**

The content contained within this book may not be reproduced, duplicated or transmitted without direct written permission from the author or the publisher.

Under no circumstances will any blame or legal responsibility be held against the publisher, or author, for any damages, reparation, or monetary loss due to the information contained within this book, either directly or indirectly.

Legal Notice:

This book is copyright protected. It is only for personal use. You cannot amend, distribute, sell, use, quote or paraphrase any part, or the content within this book, without the consent of the author or publisher.

Disclaimer Notice:

Please note the information contained within this document is for educational and entertainment purposes only. All effort has been executed to present accurate, up to date, reliable, complete information. No warranties of any kind are declared or implied. Readers acknowledge that the author is not engaged in the rendering of legal, financial, medical or professional advice. The content within this book has been derived from various sources. Please consult a licensed professional before attempting any techniques outlined in this book.

By reading this document, the reader agrees that under no circumstances is the author responsible for any losses, direct or indirect, that are incurred as a result of the use of the information contained within this document, including, but not limited to, errors, omissions, or inaccuracies.

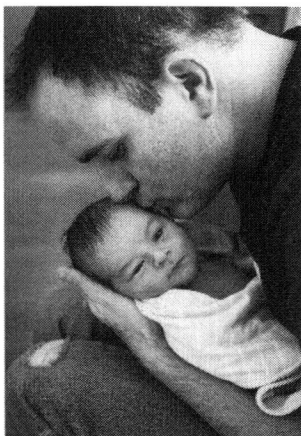

This book is dedicated to Bri, Jace, Logan, Coen, and Charli. As I watched each of you come into this world, a part of me just expanded to the point I didn't feel I could have the capacity to love as much as I love you all. I am so very proud of each of you and the people you are becoming. I promise that I will always be there for you for eternity as I am always in your heart when you need me most.

To Stephanie, I can just thank you endlessly. It has always been you that has pushed us to the point of having "our family is finally complete". God knows I would have been happy with you and multiple fur babies, but I thank you for filling my life with so much joy day in and day out. As I do miss my hair before having so many children, it has all been worth it to have the life we have together!

D.MoSon

TABLE OF CONTENTS

INTRODUCTION

It's 3 a.m., and you're cradling your newborn, trying to discern if that cry signifies hunger or fatigue. Despite feeling drained, there's an undeniable rush of emotions–a blend of exhaustion and exhilaration–that accompanies this moment. That was me not so long ago, stepping into the whirlwind adventure of fatherhood.

If you're reading this now, chances are you're teetering on the edge of one of life's most incredible journeys–fatherhood. Whether you're eagerly anticipating your baby's arrival or have recently welcomed your bundle of joy, I'm here to offer practical advice, heartfelt stories, and empowering strategies, like how to balance work, life, and self, as your trusted companion (not in a weird way), dad to dad.

I remember the first time I got the news, I was enjoying my dating life, spending the weekend scouring for concert tickets to see the Foo Fighters, when my partner entered the room, visibly upset. Concerned, I immediately inquired about what was troubling her. With tears streaming down her face, she approached me, her fear palpable, and uttered, "I think we're pregnant."

Silence enveloped the room for what felt like an eternity. Then, breaking the stillness, I managed to muster, "Okay... Okay, I wasn't expecting this," struggling to find the right words. You see, in reality, I was not okay, and saying okay over and over did not make me feel better. The truth is at that moment I was a little lost. I think my soul left my body for a second, but I quickly snapped back once I saw the distress on her face. I hugged her in a tight embrace, reassuring her, "We'll be okay. This is a blessing." And I truly believed it.

Her tears continued to flow as we talked at length, preparing ourselves for the journey ahead. Despite my initial shock, I am proud to say that I am now the father of five wonderful children-not all born at once, of course-each a testament to the unexpected turns life can take.

As a first-time father, you'll be undertaking a rapid crash course in parenting. From mastering the art of swaddling to distinguishing between hunger cries and tired whimpers, there's a great deal to absorb, kind of like a good diaper. That's precisely where this guide steps in. We'll dive into everything from the basics of diaper-changing to calming techniques, equipping you with the skills necessary to confidently care for your little one.

Let's be honest-the prospect of becoming a dad can be daunting. When my partner said those words the first time, I thought to myself "Oh shi...". But here's the inside scoop, you've got this. My mission is to bolster your confidence in your newfound role through practical tips, real-life anecdotes, and expert advice. In this guide you'll gain the reassurance needed to confront the challenges of fatherhood with courage and grace.

In today's frenetic world, balancing between work and family life can feel like you're cycling uphill. But fear not-it's not about perfect juggling; it's about discovering what works best for you and your family. From time management strategies to boundary-setting, we'll explore practical methods to cultivate harmony between your professional and personal responsibilities, ensuring your active presence and engagement in both spheres.

The end goal is straightforward yet profound: to empower you with the knowledge, skills, and confidence required to thrive in your new role. By harnessing potent parenting skills, you'll not only bond with your child but also forge deeper connections with your partner while fostering a fulfilling work-family balance. With a fusion of practical insights, personal anecdotes, and a sprinkle of humor, this guide strikes the perfect balance between being informative and entertaining. It's like sitting down with a group of seasoned dads over a cup of coffee (or whatever your preferred beverage is), swapping tales, sharing laughter, and giving advice. So, kick back, relax, and prepare to embark on the adventure of a lifetime–fatherhood awaits!

CHAPTER 1
DAD MODE UNLEASHED

GETTING YOUR MIND RIGHT WHILE NAVIGATING THE HILARIOUS HICCUPS AND HEARTFELT HIGHS OF NEW FATHERHOOD

First of all, WELCOME TO THE WILD RIDE OF FATHERHOOD! You'll soon discover that each day brings a fresh batch of surprises, laughs, and heartwarming moments. As you step into this grand adventure, holding your tiny bundle of joy for the first time, it's like stepping into a whole new universe of possibilities. In this chapter, we're diving into the mindset that will not only help you tackle the hilarious hiccups and heartfelt highs of parenthood but also celebrate the collective wisdom of fellow dads who've been there, done that, and lived to tell the tale.

You need to keep in mind that no two dads are alike, and that's what makes being a dad beautiful and awesome!

Embrace your individuality and recognize that you bring your own set of unique qualities to the table. Whether you're drawing inspiration from your upbringing or forging a new path entirely, remember that your past experiences–both the good and the not-so-good –have shaped you into the father you aspire to be.

So, take a moment to pat yourself on the back and acknowledge your strengths as a dad or dad to be. Whether you're a master diaper changer, a bedtime story aficionado, or an expert at making silly faces to elicit giggles, celebrate the skills that make you the awesome dad you are. But don't stop there–remain open to growth and new experiences. After all, fatherhood is an ever-evolving journey filled with endless opportunities for learning and development.

They say it takes a village to raise a child, but it also takes a strong partnership between you and your significant other. From partner to parent–it's a transformation unlike any other. Embrace this evolution as a wellspring of strength. It's not just your partner's pregnancy; it's yours too. Your journey toward fatherhood is a shared one, filled with moments of anticipation, excitement, and, yes, even a little bit of nervousness. But fear not because, in the end, it's all about embracing the incredible journey you're about to embark on together.

As you navigate the ups and downs of parenthood together, remember that you're in it as a unified team. Show empathy, lend a helping hand, and revel in the beautiful bond you share with your partner. Because at the end of the day, it's those heartfelt connections that make the journey of fatherhood (and parenting with your partner!) truly extraordinary.

It's completely normal to feel a mix of excitement and nervousness as you step into this unknown territory. After all, who said being a dad comes with a manual (I guess that's why this is being written, lol)? Embrace the fact that it's okay not to have all the answers right away–that's part of the adventure!

You should know that flexibility is your new best friend in the world of fatherhood. You need to be able to roll with the punches and be open to change. Sometimes, life throws curveballs, and being a father is a priority. Whether it's adjusting your schedule, rethinking your important to-do lists, or simply going with the flow—being adaptable is key to navigating this exhilarating journey.

Consider fatherhood as a lifelong learning experience. From mastering the art of soothing a crying baby to navigating the intricacies of toddler tantrums, every day brings new lessons. Get on the learning curve and allow yourself to grow and evolve as a dad with each passing moment. Set goals and aspirations for yourself as a father but remember to keep them grounded in reality. Understand that parenthood is full of surprises, and some adjustments will be necessary along the way. Regular check-ins and revisions of your goals will help you stay on track and make any needed changes as your child grows and develops.

Decide to fully commit to the adventure of fatherhood even if you think the whole thing is busted from the start. Cultivate patience and resilience as you navigate the ups and downs of this thrilling journey. There will be challenges, but with determination and a positive attitude, you'll conquer them all. So, buckle up, Dad, the ride may be unpredictable, but it's one heck of an exciting adventure!

TAPPING INTO THE EMOTIONAL ROLLERCOASTER OF NEW FATHERHOOD

As we step into the whirlwind of fatherhood, it's essential to pause and reflect on the type of father we aspire to be. In this journey, it's vital to recognize that dads, just like everyone else, are not superhuman beings—we're humans, with strengths, weaknesses, and moments of vulnerability. Accepting your human nature allows you to define how you want to be perceived in your role as a father.

The best way you can define your role and what type of a dad you want to be is to take a moment and ponder this question: "What kind of father do YOU want to be?" Answer honestly. Would you believe me if I told you that I already know the answer to your question? Well, I do. You're going to say you want to be the best dad you can be. How did I know this? Because it's all that we want to be–the best dads we can be to our children.

So, for you to be the best dad, with flaws and all, remember we're all humans; Consider the values, principles, and qualities you wish to embody as a father. How do you want your children to remember you? By envisioning the kind of father, you aspire to be, you can set a clear direction for your fatherhood journey.

Reflect on your relationship with your father. There's a wealth of wisdom to be gained from both the positive and negative aspects of their parenting. Take a realistic approach and acknowledge the elements you admire and wish to emulate, while also learning from the mistakes and shortcomings to chart your own path as a dad.

Take time to review your actions and behaviors, seeking opportunities for growth and improvement, as fatherhood is a constant learning process. Regularly evaluate your performance as a parent and don't hesitate to put yourself in check when necessary. By consistently striving to do better, you are ensuring that you're creating the best possible environment for your children to thrive.

When faced with challenges, it's essential to distinguish between reacting and responding. Instead of reacting with emotion (in the heat of the moment) or letting your anxiety dictate your actions, take a step back, a few deep breaths, and approach the situation with empathy. Keep in mind that they're still learning and developing.

As you embark on this emotional rollercoaster of new fatherhood, remember that it's okay to experience a variety of emotions. Embrace your vulnerabilities, learn from your experiences, admit when you do make mistakes and grow from them and strive to be the kind of father that your children will admire and respect for years to come.

Navigating Worries with Courage

On this journey, worries are like shadows that follow us, but it's how we face them that determines our success. As Proverbs 22:6 says: "Start children off on the way they should go, and even when they are old, they will not turn from it" (The Holy Bible: NIV, 2011). We have a guiding principle to start our children on the right path, but it's up to us to navigate the uncertainties with courage.

As fathers, we need to bear the weight of responsibilities with courage and commitment. Simply being present in our children's lives is of monumental importance. Remember, it's not about being perfect; it's about showing up and being there for our kids through thick and thin.

Yes, fatherhood comes with its fair share of fears and anxieties, from worries about miscarriages(which is heart wrenching) to concerns about providing and protecting. However, instead of letting these thoughts overwhelm us, we can approach them with curiosity and a willingness to learn and improve. Remember we are not facing the worries alone; your partner has the same concerns you have. There's also a wealth of wisdom and support available from other dads and parents who have walked this path before us. There are also numerous support groups on social media platforms, as well as in churches and communities. Don't hesitate to reach out and tap into this network of support.

While it's crucial to be present and supportive of our children, it's equally important to prioritize self-care. When we take care of ourselves, we ensure that we can be there for them for as long as possible.

Self-Care as a Superpower

In the crazy world today and with everything that comes with fatherhood, it's easy to overlook our own needs in the midst of caring for our families. Like one of our super dads realized:

> I'm Travis (father of 2) and let me tell you about the time I found out I was going to be a dad for the first time. It hit me like a ton of bricks, and not just because I was about to become a parent, but because reality smacked me right in the face. First off, I was a bit older than your average first-time dad, and I couldn't shake the image of looking more like a grandpa than a dad to my kids. And secondly, I was lugging around an extra 150 pounds, thanks to my less-than-healthy lifestyle back in the day. I used to be the king of binge-eating pizza and downing a 12-pack all by myself on a Friday night.
>
> But when I realized I was going to be responsible for a tiny human being, it scared the living daylights out of me. I knew if I kept going at that rate, I might not even be around for some of the big moments in my kid's life, let alone see them graduate high school. So, I knew I had to make a change. Becoming a parent was just the kick in the butt I needed to get my act together and start taking care of myself.
>
> Fast forward to today, I'm onto my second kid, and let me tell you, things have turned around big time. No more sleep apnea mask, no more struggling to breathe at night. I've dropped the extra weight, and I can even run a 10k without keeling over. I've

basically added a whole bunch of years to my life, all thanks to my little ones.

So, here's the deal, our kids need us. Plain and simple. And that's all the motivation I need to keep hustling and staying healthy, so I can be there for them every step of the way. Trust me, it's worth it.

Prioritizing self-care is not only crucial for our own well-being but also for our ability to be the best fathers we can be. Here's why self-care is indeed a superpower:

1. **Emotional well-being:** Fatherhood can bring a range of emotions, from immense love to moments of stress and anxiety. Taking care of ourselves emotionally means acknowledging and processing these feelings in healthy ways. This might involve finding time for hobbies or activities that bring joy, like journaling to express our thoughts, or seeking professional support if needed.
2. **Physical health:** Our physical health directly impacts our ability to care for our families. Regular medical check-ups, including screenings and vaccinations, are essential for catching any health issues early on. Additionally, similar to Travis mentioned above, maintaining a balanced diet, staying hydrated, and getting regular exercise are key components of physical self-care.
3. **Mental well-being:** The demands of fatherhood can sometimes feel overwhelming, leading to mental fatigue or even burnout. Prioritizing mental self-care involves practicing mindfulness, and stress-reduction techniques like working out or meditating, and seeking support from friends, family, or mental health professionals when needed. It's also important to recognize and respect our

own boundaries, knowing when to take breaks and recharge.

4. **Skill acquisition:** Equipping ourselves with essential skills, such as newborn CPR or basic first aid, is a proactive form of self-care. These skills not only provide us with the confidence to handle emergencies effectively but also empower us to keep our children safe.

5. **Leading by example:** By prioritizing self-care, we set a powerful example for our children. We show them the importance of valuing their own well-being and demonstrate healthy habits they can adopt and carry into adulthood.

Self-care is not selfish; it's a necessary investment in ourselves that ultimately benefits our families. By prioritizing our own emotional, physical, and mental health, we become stronger, more resilient fathers, capable of navigating the challenges of fatherhood with courage and grace. So, let's ignite that flame, lift the dumbbell, and be the best we can be!

The Mindset That Ignites Fatherhood's Flame

Becoming a father is like lighting a flame within your soul, igniting a journey filled with growth, love, and boundless possibilities. As you embark on this adventure, let your mindset be the guiding light that illuminates the path ahead.

Embrace the confidence that comes with fatherhood. You are destined to evolve into the father you're meant to be, so trust your abilities and meet the journey with courage and determination.

Your role as a father is a sacred one, filled with both challenges and triumphs. Accept the responsibilities that come with it and cherish the opportunity to shape the life of your child.

Try your best to forge a deep and meaningful connection with your child from the very beginning. Cherish the moments of bonding and let your love for them guide you through the ups and downs of fatherhood.

Take, for instance, my friend Tony's unforgettable story. Picture this: he had just returned from his honeymoon, basking in the glow of newlywed bliss, and preparing to kick off his exciting new job as a junior architect. Life seemed to be unfolding perfectly, with a loving new spouse by his side and promising career prospects on the horizon.

But then, in a moment of unexpected revelation, Tony found himself standing butt naked in the bathroom, about to hop into the shower, when his wife appeared with a mysterious object behind her back. Anticipation hung in the air as Tony's mind raced with possibilities of what was about to happen (you know, boys will be boys). Only he was met with the sight of a familiar pregnancy test, adorned with those telltale two lines.

Shock and disbelief washed over Tony as he grappled with the sudden realization of impending fatherhood. In a misguided attempt to lighten the mood, his initial reaction was a jokingly: "Is it mine?"–as soon as those words left his mouth, he felt instant regret, and grabbed his new bride in an embrace. Yet, amidst the initial shock, Tony's heart swelled with excitement and joy at the prospect of becoming a father.

As they stood there, wrapped in each other's arms, Tony and his wife shared a moment of pure, unfiltered emotion–a mix of laughter, tears, and sheer disbelief. And a few playful punches from his wife for making such a stupid joke.

Now, just when they thought they had wrapped their heads

around the idea of impending parenthood, fate threw them another curveball: they were expecting twins!

Tony's story serves as a reminder that fatherhood is full of unexpected twists and turns, but it's also a journey filled with love, laughter, and incredible moments of joy. And while each father's experience is unique, there's comfort in knowing that we're all in this together, drawing strength from the shared experiences of those who have walked this path before us.

As you step into this extraordinary adventure, embrace it with open arms. Yes, it may challenge you at times, you will make stupid jokes, but it will also bring immeasurable joy, growth, and a love that transcends time. Don't be afraid of the struggles that fatherhood brings, for the rewards are truly endless. So, let the journey begin!

CHAPTER 2
THE JOURNEY BEGINS
BUMPS, BURRITOS, AND BABY
BOOTCAMP. ARE YOU READY?

Ah, the moment when a positive pregnancy test turns a first-time dad's world upside down. Dave, a self-proclaimed burrito aficionado and avid video gamer, finds himself blissfully unaware of the life-altering news about to unfold.

As Dave lounges on the couch, happily munching on his favorite burrito, his wife, Sarah, approaches with a sly grin and a small white stick in hand. With a mix of excitement and nervousness, she presents the pregnancy test to Dave, who, in his burrito-induced haze, initially mistakes it for a fancy new game controller.

"Is this the latest of the gadget for my Xbox?" Dave asks, eyes wide with anticipation.

Sarah's amused chuckle quickly turns into a full-blown laugh as she explains the true purpose of the stick. Dave's expression shifts from confusion to disbelief as the reality of the situation sinks in.

"Wait, you mean we're having a baby?" Dave stammers, burrito forgotten as he tries to wrap his mind around the sudden revelation.

The next few moments are a blur of emotions–from shock and disbelief to sheer excitement and joy. Dave's mind races with thoughts of cribs, diapers, and late-night feedings, while Sarah can't help but giggle at her husband's adorable mix of panic and elation.

And thus begins Dave's crash course in baby boot camp–a transformative journey filled with bumps, burritos, and plenty of unexpected twists and turns.

From assembling cribs to attending birthing classes (while sneakily sneaking burritos into the hospital bag), Dave embraces the challenges and joys of impending fatherhood with gusto(and possible gas).

As the months pass and Sarah's belly grows, Dave eagerly awaits the arrival of their little bundle of joy, armed with a newfound sense of excitement and anticipation. Together, they navigate the course of pregnancy, laughing through the late-night cravings and occasional mood swings, knowing that their lives are about to change most beautifully and miraculously.

And so, with a positive pregnancy test as their catalyst, Dave and Sarah embark on the greatest adventure of all–parenthood.

UNDERSTANDING PREGNANCY: A GUIDE FOR EXPECTANT FATHERS

The period of pregnancy is nothing short of transformative. It's filled with anticipation, excitement, and a touch of nervousness–all perfectly normal emotions to experience as you prepare to become a father.

From the moment you learn about the two lines on the test, your world begins to revolve. Suddenly, your focus shifts from your own pursuits to preparing for the arrival of your precious baby.

It's a moment that's both thrilling and overwhelming, as you grapple with a whirlwind of emotions ranging from pure joy to a bit of uncertainty about what lies ahead.

As the pregnancy progresses, each milestone–from feeling those first kicks to attending baby showers–brings you closer to the reality of fatherhood. You eagerly dive into the world of parenting, devouring books, attending classes, and soaking up advice from those who've been there before.

But amidst all the excitement, there are moments of reflection. You may find yourself thinking about the kind of father you want to be, drawing inspiration from your own upbringing, and envisioning the bond you hope to share with your child.

And then, finally, the big day arrives–the day you become a dad. Holding your newborn in your arms for the first time is a moment you'll never forget. It's a flood of emotions–pride, joy, and a deep sense of love that fills every corner of your heart.

One thing most seasoned dads will tell you is how important it is to understand the physical and emotional changes your partner may experience during pregnancy. Why? Well, to support her to the best of your ability, of course. There are a plethora of books on the stages of pregnancy and you might want to grab one, if your partner hasn't already got a copy, but we want to help you from being slapped for making a dumb comment, so....Here's how you can help her go through this journey:

Physical Changes

Your partner's body will undergo numerous changes during pregnancy, from morning sickness and fatigue to weight gain and hormonal fluctuations. Be patient and understanding as she navigates these changes, offering your support and assistance whenever needed.

Dealing with Discomfort

Pregnancy-related discomfort is common and can vary from woman to woman. Educate yourself about common discomforts such as back pain, nausea, and mood swings, and be prepared to provide comfort and support as needed. Consider seeking advice from women's perspectives to gain a deeper understanding of what your partner may be experiencing.

Being an Empathetic Listener

Remember that pregnancy is possible a new experience for your partner too, and every pregnancy reacts differently. Take the time to listen to her concerns, fears, and joys without judgment. Offer a listening ear and a shoulder to lean on, providing emotional support throughout the journey.

Attending Prenatal Classes Together

Prenatal classes are a great way to learn more about pregnancy, childbirth, and newborn care. Attend these classes together to gain valuable knowledge and to show your commitment for your partner's journey.

Preparing for the Birth Plan

It's essential to have a plan in place for the birth of your child. Discuss with your partner which hospital or birthing center you will go to, who will be present during the birth, and any special preferences or requests you may have. While it may seem early to start packing, having a plan in place will help alleviate stress when the time comes. I had ours packed and ready to go two months before the due date.(and still forgot things I wanted)

Remember, pregnancy is a journey that you and your partner are embarking on together. By understanding and supporting her physical and emotional needs, attending prenatal classes, and preparing for the big day, you ensure that this special time is as smooth and enjoyable as possible for both of you.

Handling Hormonal Changes: Supporting Your Partner Through Pregnancy

Pregnancy brings about numerous hormonal changes for your partner, which can manifest in mood swings, cravings, and aversions. Believe me, this might not be the best time to try out your new dad jokes–learn to read the room. Here's how you can navigate these rough seas together:

Coping With Mood Swings

Understand that mood swings are a common and normal part of pregnancy. Be patient and supportive when your partner experiences fluctuations in mood, offering a listening ear and a reassuring presence. Sometimes, simply acknowledging her feelings can go a long way in providing comfort. On a side note, be sure to watch your tone, as a pregnant woman can detect a lack of sincerity within seconds, and the glare you will receive will be sincere! YIKES!

Managing Cravings and Aversions

Pregnancy often comes with unusual food cravings and aversions. Be flexible and accommodating when it comes to meal planning and be prepared to make extra trips to the grocery store for those unexpected cravings. Remember, your partner's dietary preferences may change frequently, so stay adaptable and open-minded. In other words, don't judge even if things get weird. My wife loved BBQ Bacon Cheeseburgers with one child, and Reese's Peanut Butter Cups with the next, while my sister loved eating pickles, and tons of ice cream for breakfast......again I say, DON'T JUDGE!

Staying Patient and Supportive

Patience is key when it comes to supporting your partner through hormonal changes. Remind yourself that these fluctuations are temporary and part of the pregnancy journey. Show your support by being understanding, empathetic, and present, even during challenging moments.

Communicating Openly

Open communication is essential during pregnancy, including discussions about intimate expectations. Hormonal changes can affect your partner's libido and comfort levels, so be respectful of her needs and preferences. Create a safe space for honest conversations about private life, ensuring that both partners feel heard and supported.

I can help you out with this little trick though. Once you are closer to your due date, and she starts dilating, this time can go fast for some and take forever for others. A little practice that started this adventure can speed up the process and induce the labor a little quicker. Wink Wink! Choose wisely young grasshopper when you decide to use this information.

Celebrating Pregnancy Milestones

Take the time to celebrate each pregnancy milestone together. From the first ultrasound to feeling the baby kick for the first time, these moments are worth cherishing and commemorating. Plan special outings or activities to mark these occasions and reflect on the journey you're embarking on together.

Approach this time of hormonal changes with understanding, patience, and open communication. So, you can support your partner through the ups and downs of pregnancy. Remember to celebrate each milestone along the way and appreciate the unique bond you share with your loved one as you prepare to welcome your new arrival. However, don't stop there and support your partner in keeping her health in check during this time.

Navigating Health and Wellness During Pregnancy: A Guide for Expectant Fathers

Ensuring the health and well-being of your partner and the unborn child is a top priority during pregnancy. Let's dive in and look at how you can do that.

Encouraging a Healthy Lifestyle

Promote a healthy lifestyle by encouraging your partner to prioritize regular exercise, balanced nutrition, and adequate rest. Offer to join her for walks or prenatal yoga sessions to stay active together. Additionally, provide emotional support and encouragement to help her maintain a positive mindset. Don't think you can't exercise, as my wife was riding a bike, and running up into the 3rd trimester. Just consult with your doctor on what is best for your partner and the baby.

Prenatal Vitamins and Nutrition

Encourage your partner to take prenatal vitamins and maintain a balanced diet. Vitamins are crucial for the healthy development of the baby and can help prevent certain birth defects such as low birth weight, preterm, or neural tube defects. Encourage her to consume a variety of fruits, vegetables, lean proteins, and whole grains to ensure she's getting essential macro- and micronutrients from the diet.

Managing Pregnancy Complications

Be prepared to navigate any potential pregnancy complications that may arise. Stay informed about common complications such as gestational diabetes, preeclampsia, or placenta previa, and work closely with your partner's healthcare provider to monitor them.

Remember, you and your partner are a team when it comes to health and wellness during pregnancy. Encourage a healthy lifestyle and support her in taking prenatal vitamins and nutrition. Also, keep yourself up to date with the signs of any complications should your partner experience any. And, of course, be prepared to address any complications. This can help ensure a smooth and healthy pregnancy.

Now, let's get a little more hands-on and get some stuff done around the home.

TOOL TIME DAD-GETTIN R DONE

Alright, let's talk about choosing the right baby products—I know it's like stepping into a whole new world filled with endless options and possibilities. But fear not, because I've got your back.

When it comes to picking out baby products, there are a few key things to keep in mind:

Do Your Research

With so many baby products on the market, it's essential to do your homework. Read reviews, ask for recommendations from friends and family, and check out parenting forums and websites for advice. You want to make sure you're investing in products that are safe, durable, and well-regarded by other parents. At the same time, do not get lost in the commercial marketing that is all directed at new parents. You DO NOT NEED everything! Ask other dads and parents what they actually used that first year. I guarantee there are several things that I used once and then just didn't want to mess with it afterward. One thing that comes to mind is the baby changing station. You're not going to walk the baby to the nursery to change the "blowout." I sprayed my baby down in our kitchen sink before I went upstairs to that changing station. Yes, that really happened and worked amazingly!

Consider Your Lifestyle

Think about your lifestyle and what products will best fit into it. Are you always on the go? Look for lightweight and portable strollers and car seats. Do you have limited space at home? Opt for compact baby gear that can easily be folded or stored away when not in use.

Budget Wisely

While it can be tempting to splurge on every cute baby gadget you see, it's essential to stick to your budget. Prioritize the must-have items–like a safe crib, car seat, and diapers–and save the splurges for special occasions.

Safety First

When it comes to baby products, safety is non-negotiable. Look for items that meet safety standards and have been tested for durability and reliability. Check for any recalls or safety warnings before making a purchase.

Think Long-Term

Babies grow fast, so consider how long you'll be able to use each product. Look for items that can grow with your child or serve multiple purposes to get the most bang for your buck. One such examples would be a crib that can convert to a toddler bed, and then full size bed for your child.

Keep in mind, that choosing the right products is all about finding what works best for you and your family. Trust your instincts, do your research, and don't be afraid to ask for advice along the way. With a little bit of preparation and some savvy shopping skills, you'll be ready to tackle baby products like a pro!

Setting up a Nursery

Ah, setting up the nursery, creating a cozy little nest for your soon-to-arrive little darling Kind of reminds me of a story I heard from another dad.

So, there's Dave(now father of 3), the soon-to-be dad, on a mission to set up the nursery for his impending bundle of joy. Armed with determination and a questionable DIY skillset (his wife's words, not mine), he dives headfirst into the task at hand.

With boxes of baby gear stacked to the ceiling, Dave feels like he's about to conquer Mount Everest. But as he cracks open the instruction manual for the crib, he quickly realizes he's in for a wild ride. Screws go missing, parts refuse to cooperate, and Dave finds himself in a tangled mess of wood and confusion. It's like trying to solve a Rubik's Cube blindfolded–frustrating and utterly baffling.

After a moment of panic (and maybe a few choice words muttered under his breath), Dave turns to the internet for help. He stumbles upon a forum for DIY dads, where he commiserates with fellow fathers who've been through the nursery setup gauntlet.

With newfound confidence (and a healthy dose of humor), Dave jumps back into the fray. Hours fly by as he wrestles with the crib, but eventually, victory is his–the crib stands tall and sturdy, a testament to his DIY prowess.

But Dave's triumph is short-lived. As he attempts to install the baby monitor, disaster strikes–he accidentally drills into a water pipe, unleashing a mini-flood in the nursery. Cue the panic!

Luckily, Dave's wife walks in just in time to witness the chaos. Instead of getting mad, they share a good laugh over the nursery setup shenanigans, knowing that parenthood is all about embracing the unexpected.

In the end, Dave and his wife realize that no matter how many disasters they face, they're in this together—one screw-up at a time. And as they sit amidst the wreckage of their nursery, they know that they're ready to take on whatever parenthood throws their way—soggy carpets and all!

Alright, now let's dive into how to make the nursery the perfect space for your new addition:

Choose a Theme or Color Scheme

Start by deciding on a theme or color scheme for the nursery. Whether you're going for a classic look, a whimsical theme, or something unique, pick a palette that reflects your style and creates a soothing atmosphere for your baby.

Select Essential Furniture

The nursery will need some key pieces of furniture, including a crib, a dresser, and a comfortable rocking chair or glider for late-night feedings and snuggles. Make sure to choose furniture that is safe, sturdy, and meets current safety standards. Add soft furnishings like rugs, curtains, and bedding to make the nursery feel cozy and inviting. Opt for materials that are gentle on baby's skin and easy to clean, and don't forget to add some decorative touches to personalize the space.

Organize Storage Solutions

Although small, babies can quickly accumulate a lot of stuff (maybe it's the cuteness), so it's essential to have plenty of storage options in the nursery. Consider adding shelves, baskets, or bins for storing diapers, wipes, clothes, toys, and other baby essentials. Keeping everything organized will make life much easier once your little one arrives.

Create a Safe Sleep Environment

Safety is paramount especially when it comes to creating a safe sleeping environment for your baby. Avoid using loose bedding, stuffed animals, or crib bumpers, which can pose suffocation hazards.

Setting up the nursery is an exciting part of preparing for your new arrival. Take your time, enjoy the process, and let your creativity shine as you design a special space for your little one to grow and thrive. Add some personal touches to the nursery to make it feel like home. Hang family photos, artwork, or letters spelling out your baby's name on the wall to add warmth and character to the room.

Baby Essentials Checklist

Let's be honest–preparing for your baby's arrival can be overwhelming with lists and lists and lists of things you "simply have to get." And believe me, friends and family will all be too eager to pile on to that list and get you stuff that you don't even know what it's for (I don't think they even know what it's for either).

Take a changing table, for example, a great gift, and it comes in handy, but once you're in the diaper-changing game, you'll soon realize that the perfect game plan is to have "changing stations" strategically placed throughout the house. Believe me, you don't always have the time or the energy to run to the nursery.

Here's a basic baby essentials checklist to help you prepare for your little one's arrival:

Nursery:

- Crib or bassinet
- Mattress and waterproof mattress cover
- Fitted crib sheets
- Dresser
- Rocking chair or glider
- Baby monitor
- Night light
- Blackout curtains or blinds
- Diaper pail (a diaper genie or equivalent is your friend)

Feeding:

- Bottles (4-8 ounce)
- Bottlebrush
- Formula or breastfeeding supplies (nursing bras, breast pads, nipple cream)
- Bottle warmer or bottle sterilizer (if using bottles)
- Burp cloths (kitchen towel works perfectly fine when you're in a pinch)
- Highchair or booster seat (for later stages – you have time)

Diapering:

- Diapers (newborn size and not used very long so get staggered sizes)
- Wipes
- Diaper rash cream
- Diaper bag
- Portable changing pad

Clothing:

- Onesies (short and long-sleeved)
- Sleepers or footed pajamas
- Swaddle blankets
- Hats and mittens (for colder weather and mittens are great to stop scratching)
- Socks or booties
- Baby towels and washcloths

Health and Safety:

- Infant car seat (properly installed, more on this in Chapter 8)
- Stroller or baby carrier
- Baby bathtub
- Baby grooming kit (nail clippers, thermometer, bulb syringe)
- Baby first aid kit (saline drops, infant acetaminophen, baby sunscreen)
- Outlet covers (once they are on the move – again you have time)
- Cabinet locks (same as outlet covers)
- Baby gate (if needed)

Playtime and Development:

- Baby swing or bouncer
- Play mat or activity gym
- Soft toys or rattles
- Teething toys
- Baby mirror for car

Miscellaneous:

- Pacifiers (if desired)
- Nursing pillow (if breastfeeding)
- Baby laundry detergent
- Infant toiletries (gentle soap, shampoo, lotion)

Remember, every baby is different, so you may find that you need to adjust this checklist based on your family's specific needs and preferences. Additionally, don't feel pressured to buy everything at once–focus on the essentials and gradually add items as you need them. This is also where budgeting and some financial planning help.

BUDGETING AND FINANCIAL PLANNING

Parenthood brings with it a host of new expenses, from diapers and baby gear to childcare and healthcare costs. Take some time to assess your current financial situation and estimate how much these new expenses will impact your budget. Considering factors such as changes in income (due to parental leave or reduced work hours), increased healthcare costs, and the need for additional savings.

Creating a Baby Budget

Before getting down into the nitty gritty, take stock of your current financial situation by making a list of all your monthly expenses, including:

- rent or mortgage payments
- utilities
- groceries
- transportation costs

- insurance premiums
- debt payments
- entertainment expenses
- any other regular bills

Then deduct them from your monthly income to determine your disposable income and what you have to play with.

Factor in new Expenses

Once you have a clear picture of your current finances, it's time to add in the new expenses associated with having a baby. Some common baby expenses to consider can include:

1. **Diapers and wipes:** A big part of your budget will go toward these essentials. Once your baby has arrived, you'll quickly get a clear picture of how many diapers they go through in a month.
2. **Formula or breastfeeding supplies:** When breastfeeding, you may want to consider any additional supplies your partner might need such as a breast pump and nursing bras.
3. **Baby gear:** These are big ticket items like a crib, stroller, car seat, and highchair, as well as smaller items like baby clothes, blankets, and toys.
4. **Childcare:** If you and your partner plan to return to work after the baby is born, childcare costs can be significant. Make sure to do some research and compare the costs of daycare centers, in-home daycare providers, or hiring a nanny.
5. **Healthcare costs:** This may include expenses like pediatrician visits, vaccinations, and any out-of-pocket expenses that are not covered by your insurance.

Budget for the Unexpected

In addition to budgeting for regular baby-related expenses, it's very important to set aside a little something for unexpected expenses and emergencies. Just like life, babies can be unpredictable, and you don't want to be caught off guard by emergency medical expenses, or other things like car repairs, or sudden home repairs. Aim to have a buffer of at least a few hundred dollars in your budget to cover unexpected costs.

Review and Adjust

After going through all of that, the fun is not over yet. Regularly review and adjust your budget in real time, keep track of what you're spending each month and compare it to your budgeted amounts. If you find that you're consistently overspending in certain areas, you may need to adjust your budget or spending accordingly. Of course, if your income or expenses change significantly, be sure to update your budget.

Creating a baby budget may seem daunting to near impossible at first. Like assembling that crib with vague instructions, with no pictures, and a few missing screws. However, you'll quickly get the hang of it, don't stew. With careful planning and attention to detail, you will ensure that you're financially prepared for the arrival of your little one.

Long-Term Financial Planning

Parenthood is a long-term commitment, so it's crucial to think about your family's financial future. Consider saving for your child's education with a 529 college savings plan or other education savings account. Review your retirement savings goals and consider how parenthood may impact your plans. It's never too early to start planning for your family's long-term financial security.

By assessing your financial situation, creating a budget, and planning for both the expected and unexpected expenses of parenthood, you can set yourself up for financial success as you embark on this new chapter of your life. Remember, being proactive about your finances now will pay off in the long run and help ensure a bright future for your growing family.

PARENTING WORKSHOPS AND CLASSES

So, let's talk about parenting workshops and classes–they're like crash courses for soon-to-be or new parents. You know, those places where they teach you all the baby basics, from how to change a diaper without making a mess to soothing a crying baby without losing your mind. But they're not just about the practical stuff; they're also great for meeting other expectant parents who are going through the same wild ride as you.

Here's why you should consider hopping on the parenting class bandwagon:

1. **Get schooled:** These classes are like Parenting 101, covering everything from birth to baby care. You'll come out feeling like a pro, ready to tackle whatever parenthood throws your way.
2. **Team bonding:** It's not just about learning–it's also about bonding with your partner. Working together to soak up all that knowledge can strengthen your relationship and get you both pumped up for the adventure ahead.
3. **Meet your tribe:** Ever heard the saying, "It takes a village to raise a child"? Well, these classes are where you'll find your tribe–other parents who get what you're going through and can offer support and solidarity.

4. **Expert advice:** You'll get tips and tricks from the pros—think experienced nurses, pediatricians, and baby whisperers who know their stuff. They'll arm you with all the info you need to feel confident and prepared.

5. **Local connections:** Plus, these classes are like a treasure trove of local resources. They'll hook you up with info on everything from pediatricians to playgroups, so you'll always know where to turn for help and support.

So, as you wrap up this chapter, remember that getting ready for fatherhood isn't just about cramming your brain full of facts—it's about gearing up for the crazy, wonderful ride ahead. You're laying the groundwork for a journey filled with love, laughter, and plenty of unforgettable moments. And don't worry—you've got this!

CHAPTER 3
PUSHING LIMITS AND DAD JOKES

A FIRST-TIME DAD'S EXPEDITION INTO THE DELIVERY ROOM

The experience of welcoming each child into the world is unique and unforgettable, but there's something truly special about the first time. Let me share a glimpse into my own journey as a first-time dad:

I thought I was prepared. I had read all the books, seen medical procedures in the military from a medical assistant perspective, and felt like I had a good handle on what to expect. But when it came down to it, nothing could have prepared me for the wave of emotions that accompanied the birth of our first child.

As my wife was given "Pitocin" to induce labor, our excitement quickly turned to concern when our baby's heart rate started fluctuating erratically. What was supposed to be a natural birth suddenly became a potential C-section, and the anxiety in the room skyrocketed–mine included.

However, in those tense moments, I knew I had to stay strong for my wife. I reassured her that everything would be okay, even though my own heart was racing a mile a minute. Thankfully, when they decided to stop the Pitocin, our baby's heart rate stabilized, and we were able to proceed with our original birthing plan.

In the end, we welcomed our amazing baby boy into the world, and despite the unexpected twists and turns, everything turned out just fine. It was a reminder that no matter how much you plan, sometimes life has other ideas–and all you can do is stay sane and keep calm in the face of uncertainty.

So, soon-to-be dad, remember this: while you may not have all the answers, your presence and support mean everything to your partner. Trust the doctors, have faith in yourself, and the rest is in God's hands. Embrace the journey because, in the end, the joy of holding your newborn in your arms makes every moment of uncertainty worth it.

THE DELIVERY ROOM-THINGS TO DO AND NOT TO DO

The delivery room–a place where excitement and nerves collide as you eagerly await the arrival of your little one. But before you dive headfirst into the chaos of childbirth, there are a few things you should know about what to do and what not to do.

1. **Provide Support:** Remember, you're the cheerleader, not the coach. Your key responsibility is to support your partner every step of the way. Have a chat beforehand to find out what she expects from you and know your limitations–if blood makes you squeamish, it's okay to stick by her head.
2. **Be an Advocate:** Advocate for your partner's needs and preferences during labor. Whether it's advocating for pain relief options or ensuring her wishes are respected, your voice matters in the delivery room.

3. **Capture Precious Moments:** Want to record the magical moment of your baby's arrival? Just make sure to ask your partner before you hit record. And remember, newborns don't exactly come out looking like the Gerber baby–be prepared for a bit of a surprise!

4. **Handle Unexpected Situations:** Be flexible, because let's face it–shit happens. Literally. From unexpected poops to unforeseen complications, stay calm and roll with the punches.

5. **Assisting During Labor:** Stay calm under pressure–you're not a football coach rallying the team. Keep your tone low and soothing, offering encouragement and support to your partner as she navigates labor pains.

6. **Cutting the Umbilical Cord:** It's your moment to shine as you cut the umbilical cord, but don't worry, you won't screw it up. Just be prepared for a bit of resistance–the cord is thick and spongy, making it a bit tricky to cut. Take a deep breath, steady your hand, and cut with confidence. On a side note: the way you cut the cord will not determine if your child has an "innie" vs an "outie" belly button, as that is based on how the cord heals, so cut away!

7. **Bonding With the Newborn:** Once your little one arrives, take the opportunity to bond with them. Skin-to-skin contact, gentle touches, and speaking softly can all help foster that special connection between you and your baby.

8. **Sharing the Joy:** After the dust settles and your baby is safely in your arms, share and hold onto those first moments with your partner. Take a deep breath and just simply take it all in. The family photos and social media updates can wait till later. This is your new little family time together so cherish every second possible.

Now, let's talk about what your newborn won't look like. Forget those picture-perfect images you see in magazines, like the one below—the reality might be a bit different.

Just ask Allen, father of three, who admits to having a moment of confusion when he saw his first daughter's pointy head and hairy back as she made her entrance into the world.

So, let me tell you about the first time I saw my daughter enter the world. Honestly, I wasn't expecting her to come out looking like she just stepped off a magazine cover. Nope, she had a bit more character than that.

As she made her way into the world, I couldn't help but have this look of confusion mixed with curiosity on my face. She had more hair than I anticipated, her head was a bit pointy, and to top it off, she even had some fuzz on her back—just like dear old dad.

When my wife asked if she was okay, I quickly adjusted my expression and proudly declared, "She's beautiful." And you know what? Despite the initial shock, she truly was—hairy back and all.

With time, those little quirks faded away, leaving behind the most precious little girl I could ever imagine. So, to all you soon-to-be dads out there, be prepared for anything when your little one arrives. Because no matter what surprises come your way, the love you feel for your child will always shine through.

You see, while you might have this picture-perfect image in your head of what your newborn will look like, reality might be a bit different.

Take it from me as you're getting that front-row view of your baby's arrival, as your partner might not have the same perspective. She'll be relying on the look on your face to gauge how everything's going–and trust me, the last thing you want to do is freak her out for no reason.

So, when you catch that first glimpse of your little one, keep calm and keep it cool. The image below will give you a better idea of what your baby might look like. Remember, every baby is unique and beautiful in their own way, and your partner will be taking their cues from you. So, put on your best poker face, and get ready to welcome your bundle of joy into the world with a smile.

cone-shaped head from
squeezing through the womb

Puffy, bloodshot eyes

Flat nose and off-centered
chin from womb pressure

Lanugo - fuzzy
hair on face, back
& shoulders

Genitals may be
swollen
but will shrink
back down

Umbilical cord will remain
after you cut it then will
fall off in a few days

Skinny, structually
unsound legs

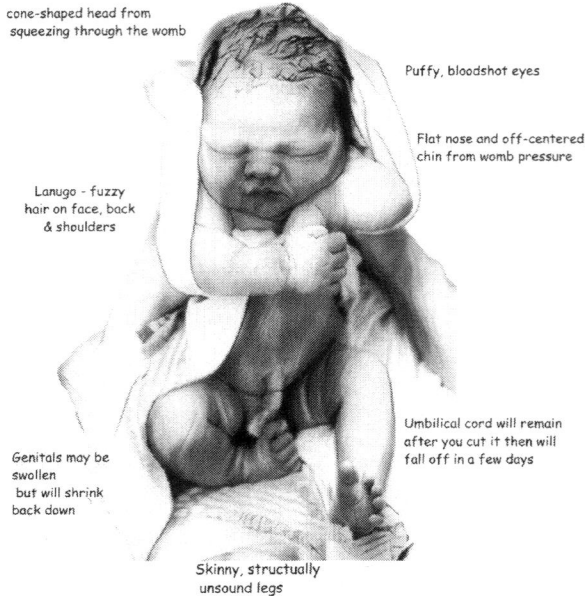

Another amazing experience, they do not share in the movies, is the "after birth" also called the Placenta expulsion. This happens after childbirth when the placenta comes out of the birth canal, also referred as the third stage of labor. Usually your partner will have to push a few more times to help the doctor support the expulsion, and I'll be honest, it really isn't anything you want to watch unless you truly and are curious. I saw this with my first child and then focused on the baby and cutting the cord during this stage with all my others. Remember, childbirth is a team effort, and your active participation can make all the difference in creating a positive and memorable experience for both you and your partner. So, take a deep breath, roll up your sleeves, and get ready to welcome your little one into the world with open arms and a heart full of love.

"BABY ON BOARD"–BRING YOUR BABY HOME

Buckle up, folks! It's time to bring your little bundle of joy home and dive headfirst into the wonderful world of parenthood. Make sure as you get closer to your due date, just like that prepared suitcase, you also have the car seat base and carrier already in your vehicle, strapped and ready for the drive home. It's important to know that all U.S. hospitals will make sure you have a rear-facing car seat before allowing you to leave.

Now, let's talk about creating the perfect cozy nest for your newborn. First up, soft blankets. Think of them as fluffy clouds ready to cradle your baby in comfort. Whether it's a snuggly swaddle for bedtime or a cozy throw for nap time, soft fabrics are a must-have for your baby's ultimate comfort.

Soft, diffused light can work wonders in creating a calming atmosphere. Consider using dimmer switches or soft lampshades to create a warm glow that's perfect for those late-night cuddle sessions.

And don't forget about soothing sounds. Whether it's the gentle hum of a white noise machine or a playlist of soothing tunes, background noise can help your baby drift off to dreamland and create a peaceful environment for everyone in the house.

Baby's First Days at Home

Those first days at home with your newborn are a precious time filled with wonder, joy, and a whole lot of new experiences.

First and foremost, get ready for some sleepless nights and round-the-clock feedings. Your little one's schedule will be unpredictable at first, and it's normal to feel a bit overwhelmed. But remember, you're not alone–every parent has been there, and you'll quickly find your rhythm as you bond with your baby.

It's also a time of getting to know each other. You'll marvel at every little yawn, squeak, and stretch as you discover your baby's personality and preferences. And don't be surprised if you find yourself staring in awe at your tiny miracle for hours on end–that's just part of the magic of parenthood. I don't think I could count how many times my wife would state in miraculous glee, "We made that"!

The first days at home with your newborn are a thrilling yet challenging time for new dads. Here are some tips to help you navigate this exciting journey and make the transition as smooth as possible:

1. **Create a Comfortable Environment:** Set up a cozy and safe space for your baby to sleep, play, and relax. Ensure the nursery or sleeping area is equipped with essential items as we talked about in the previous chapter. Keep the room temperature comfortable and free from any hazards.

2. **Support Your Partner:** Your partner will be recovering from childbirth and adjusting to the demands of caring for a newborn. Offer emotional support, lend a helping hand with household chores, and encourage her to rest whenever possible. Remember, you're in this together, and teamwork makes all the difference.

3. **Learn the Basics of Baby Care:** Take the time to familiarize yourself with essential baby care tasks, such as diaper changing, bathing, feeding, and soothing techniques. This is where those parenting classes or workshops come in handy.

4. **Be Hands-On:** Embrace your role as an active and involved dad from the start. Take on diaper duty, participate in feeding sessions, and engage in bonding activities like skin-to-skin contact and cuddling.

5. **Bond with Your Baby:** Building a strong bond with your newborn is crucial for their emotional development and your relationship with them. Spend quality time together, talk to your baby, sing lullabies, and read stories. These simple gestures can strengthen the bond between you and your little one. Honestly, I really didn't know too many lullabies, so at times I would be humming my favorite rock ballads and it worked amazingly!

6. **Practice Patience:** Parenthood is full of surprises, and it's normal to feel crazy or uncertain at times. Be patient with yourself, your partner, and your baby as you adjust to your new roles and routines. This is even more important these first weeks as your adjusting to your sleep deprivation and maybe a *little* cranky. Remember that it's okay to seek support from friends, family, or healthcare professionals if you need guidance or some advice.

7. **Prioritize Self-Care:** Amidst the demands of caring for a newborn, don't forget to prioritize your own and your partner's well-being. Get plenty of rest whenever possible, eat nutritious meals, stay hydrated, and make time for activities that help you relax and recharge. Taking care of yourself allows you to be the best dad you can be for your baby. This may sound bad, but make sure you take time for showers or a bath. These may be the most relaxing showers ever, just don't fall asleep (noted from experience)!

The key is that you and your partner need to create a nurturing environment together and support each other. It is important to learn the essential skills for taking care of a baby but the best way to learn is to be hands-on and be patient. Plus, the more time you spend together the more you bond.

Setting a Routine

Setting a routine for your newborn is essential for establishing a sense of predictability and stability in their early days. While newborns don't follow strict schedules like adults, creating a flexible routine can help you and your baby adjust to daily life at home. Here's how you can set a routine for your newborn.

Feeding Schedule

Newborns typically need to eat every 2-3 hours, so feeding your baby on demand (called responsive feeding) is essential during the early weeks. As your baby grows and their feeding patterns become more predictable, you can gradually establish a feeding schedule. Whether your partner is breastfeeding or formula feeding, aim to feed your baby whenever they show hunger cues, such as rooting or sucking on their fists. This sometimes for breastfeeding moms may mean they need to pump and store milk for later, which gives dad the opportunity to help in some of the feedings.

Sleep Routine

Newborns spend most of their time sleeping, but their sleep patterns can be irregular and unpredictable. Help your baby differentiate between day and night by keeping daytime feedings and interactions lively and engaging, while nighttime feedings should be quiet and calm. Establish a bedtime routine that includes activities like a warm bath, gentle massage, and soothing lullabies to signal to your baby that it's time to wind down and prepare for sleep.

Diaper Changes: Beware of the Poo

Diaper changes are an inevitable part of caring for a newborn. While there's no set schedule for changing diapers, aim to check your baby's diaper regularly and change it whenever it's wet or soiled. Incorporate diaper changes into your baby's routine before or after feedings, naps, and bedtime to ensure they stay clean and comfortable.

As a forewarning, do not freak out when you see your newborn's first poop. That thick, tarry, black yucky mess is called meconium and is basically the poo accumulated from umbilical feeding before birth. Also, poo is different for breastfed babies vs. formula fed. The all-mighty boob-fed babies will produce a mustard yellow poop, while the Formula 1 baby will be more pasty brown. This change in poo color is a good thing as it will let you know they are getting plenty to eat.

Playtime and Interaction

Even though newborns spend much of their time sleeping, they also benefit from short periods of wakefulness and interaction during the day. Engage your baby in gentle playtime activities, such as talking, singing, and cuddling, to promote bonding and stimulate their senses. Keep play sessions brief and follow your baby's cues for when they need rest or stimulation.

Monitor Your Baby's Cues

Pay close attention to your baby's cues and signals, such as hunger cues, tiredness, and discomfort. Respond promptly to their needs and adapt your routine accordingly. Remember that every baby is unique, so be flexible and willing to adjust your schedule based on your newborn's individual preferences and development.

Here are just a few "party tricks" you can do to monitor their reflexes while you are playing:

- **Babinski:** When you touch the sole of the baby's foot their toes fan out and the foot twists in.
- **Grasping:** Touch the palm and newborns will grasp tightly.
- **Stepping:** An infant held above a surface and gently lowered to touch the surface will move its feet as if it's walking. No, your baby isn't gifted and going to the Olympics any time soon, this is just a reflex, sorry!
- **Rooting:** Stroke the baby's cheek or side of the mouth and the child will turn their head, open their mouth, and begin sucking in search of eating.

Setting a routine for your newborn may take time and patience, but consistency and predictability can help your baby feel secure and content. Be gentle with yourself and your baby as you navigate the early days of parenthood and trust your instincts as you establish a routine that works best for your family.

Managing Visitors

Ah, the influx of well-meaning friends and family members! While we're thrilled to show off our new addition, it's important to set boundaries. When it comes to visitors, remember to prioritize the baby's health and well-being.

Providing Access

When welcoming visitors, it's important to prioritize the health and well-being of the baby. Ask all visitors to wash their hands thoroughly before holding the baby, as clean hands can help prevent the spread of germs. Encourage visitors to relax and remain calm around the baby, as babies can pick up on stress cues (yes, they can smell fear). If a visitor seems uncomfortable or unsure, suggest they take a seat and hold the baby with their arms crossed over their lap to ensure a secure hold.

Denying Access

Trust your instincts when it comes to allowing visitors to interact with your newborn. If a visitor's behavior or condition raises concerns, it's okay to politely decline their visit. You can use creative excuses to politely turn down visitors, such as mentioning that the baby is allergic to certain scents or substances or expressing concerns about the visitor's appearance or behavior. You can always have the excuse ready for drunk Uncle Timmy that the baby has been having really bad diarrhea so you're just making sure his polyester shirt doesn't get ruined! Remember, your priority is the health and safety of your baby, so don't hesitate to set boundaries with visitors as needed.

Learning Baby Cues & fun Party Tricks

Understanding your baby's cues and discovering fun party tricks is an exciting aspect of parenthood that allows you to connect deeply with your little one and better understand their needs. Babies communicate through various cues, including crying, facial expressions, body movements, and sounds. By observing and interpreting these cues, you can learn to respond to your baby's needs more effectively. For instance, a hungry baby may root or suck on their fists, while a tired baby may rub their eyes or yawn. Recognizing and responding to these cues fosters a strong bond and promotes a sense of security for your baby.

Bonding activities play a crucial role in strengthening the connection between you and your baby while supporting their development. Spend quality time engaging in activities such as talking, singing, cuddling, and playing. These interactions provide valuable sensory stimulation and help nurture emotional attachment. Experiment with different activities to discover what resonates most with your baby and incorporate them into your daily routine. One of the most enjoyable activities I used to do with my babies is what I like to call "Can You Hear Me Now." It's a simple game that doesn't even have an official name, but it's loads of fun! Basically, I would stroll around the room making silly noises, and sure enough, my little one would turn their head toward the sounds. Not only is it entertaining, but it's also great for developing their ability to track sounds and sights. Plus, it sets the stage for classic games like Peekaboo and Hide & Seek, adding even more excitement to playtime!

As your baby grows and develops, you'll witness a range of delightful party tricks that showcase their emerging skills and personality. From adorable smiles and giggles to reaching for objects and rolling over, each milestone is a cause for celebration. Encourage your baby's development by providing age-appropriate toys and activities that stimulate their senses and encourage exploration. Celebrate each new achievement with praise and affection, fostering positive reinforcement for your baby's efforts.

Building confidence as a parent involves trusting your instincts and responding sensitively to your baby's needs. This creates a sense of security and trust between you and your little one. Every baby is unique, so embrace the journey of discovering what works best for you and your new family member. Enjoy the precious moments of connection and discovery as you navigate parenthood together with curiosity, patience, and love.

FEEDING AND NUTRITION: THE BOOB OR NOT THE BOOB, THAT IS THE QUESTION

Feeding and nutrition are essential aspects of caring for your newborn, and there are various considerations to keep in mind to ensure your baby's health and well-being.

Breastfeeding is hailed as the gold standard for infant nutrition due to its numerous benefits. Breast milk provides essential nutrients, antibodies, and hormones that support your baby's growth and development while offering protection against infections and diseases. Additionally, breastfeeding promotes bonding between the mother and baby and has numerous health advantages for both such as:

1. **Ideal Nutrition:** Breast milk delivers a precise blend of nutrients crucial for the initial six months of life, adjusting to meet the evolving needs of your baby.
2. **Antibodies:** Particularly in the early stages, breast milk, notably colostrum, is rich in antibodies that safeguard your baby against infections and illnesses.
3. **Enhanced Growth:** Research indicates that breastfed infants tend to experience improved health outcomes, boasting higher intelligence scores and reduced risks of obesity and diabetes in their later years (Breastfeeding, 2019).

However, breastfeeding may not be feasible or suitable for every family. Some mothers may encounter challenges such as latching difficulties, low milk supply, or medical conditions that make breastfeeding impractical. In such cases, formula feeding can provide a viable alternative. Formula milk is specially formulated to mimic the composition of breast milk, providing essential nutrients necessary for your baby's growth and development.

When it comes to feeding methods, both breastfeeding and bottle-feeding have their pros and cons. Breastfeeding offers convenience, cost savings, and health benefits for both mother and baby. On the other hand, bottle-feeding allows for greater flexibility and may involve other family members, including dads, in the feeding process. Ultimately, the decision between breastfeeding and formula feeding depends on what works best for your family's circumstances and preferences.

As a dad, there are many ways you can support your partner with feeding, regardless of whether she chooses to breastfeed or bottle-feed. You can assist with preparing formula milk, sterilizing bottles, and feeding the baby during nighttime wakeups to allow your partner to rest. Additionally, you can offer emotional support and encouragement to your partner, especially during challenging moments.

Jerry, a father of two, shares a valuable tip for parents who are breastfeeding and using a pump: make sure to date and rotate your milk supply. "I would FIFO (First In First Out) all of our milk to assure freshness". Breast milk can be stored in the freezer and remains best within 6 months but can still be used for up to a year! By pumping and storing breast milk, Jerry and his family were able to save a significant amount of money. However, it's essential to stay organized and rotate your milk supply to prevent any waste. In fact, they had so much leftover milk that once their children transitioned away from breastfeeding, they were able to sell the surplus online for a surprising price of $1.50 per ounce! When I heard this I searched myself and I've seen significantly higher and some lower prices, but it's incredible what you can achieve with a little organization and planning.

Establishing a feeding schedule can help provide structure and consistency for you and your baby. As mentioned before, newborns typically feed every 2-3 hours, although individual feeding patterns may vary. Pay attention to your baby's hunger cues, such as rooting, sucking motions, or crying, and respond promptly to their needs. Remember that feeding is not just about nourishment but also an opportunity for bonding and connection with your little one.

SLEEP STRATEGIES

Newborn sleep follows a distinct pattern characterized by short sleep cycles and frequent waking periods. Most newborns sleep for 16-17 hours a day, often in short stretches of 2-4 hours at a time. It's essential to create a sleep-friendly environment for your baby, with a comfortable sleep surface, appropriate room temperature, and minimal disturbances.

As your baby grows, you may explore sleep training techniques to help establish healthy sleep habits. These techniques, such as the "cry it out" method or gentle sleep training, aim to teach your baby to self-soothe and settle themselves to sleep independently. It's essential to choose a method that aligns with your parenting style and your baby's temperament.

Co-sleeping, or sharing a bed with your baby, is a personal choice that comes with both benefits and risks. While co-sleeping can facilitate bonding and breastfeeding, it's crucial to practice safe sleep practices to reduce the risk of accidents, such as suffocation or Sudden Infant Death Syndrome (SIDS).

Safe sleep practices include monitoring light and darkness to regulate your baby's circadian rhythm, establishing "wake windows" to promote daytime wakefulness, and ensuring your baby stays awake during feedings to prevent sleep association with feeding.

Managing sleep regressions, periods when your baby's sleep patterns are temporarily disrupted can be challenging but temporary. Common sleep regressions occur around 4 months, 6 months, and 9-12 months of age and may be triggered by developmental milestones, teething, or changes in routine. Consistency, patience, and reassurance can help your baby navigate these transitions more smoothly.

Some of you might be sitting there after reading this chapter and thinking, "Wow, this is a lot to take in," while others might find it all to be common sense. And you know what? That's perfectly okay! Parenting comes naturally to some, while for others, it can feel like a never-ending rollercoaster of anxiety. But here's the thing: no matter how you feel, just enjoy the ride, you are going to pull through!

Every seasoned father will tell you to cherish these moments because they fly by in the blink of an eye. And you know what? That is 100% true! Those first few months with your baby are going to be a whirlwind of rapid development and discoveries every single day. So, take it all in, snap tons of pictures, and record videos of those precious moments.

Sure, you're going to make mistakes along the way, but that's all part of the journey. Laugh at those mishaps, learn from them, and keep moving forward. Remember to support each other with your partner through the sleepless nights and exhausting days because, trust me, there will be plenty of those!

Dedicate your time, cherish every moment, and before you know it, you'll look back and realize just how quickly they grow up. You got this dads!

CHAPTER 4
BUBBLY WRAP AND BOO-BOOS

THE DELICATE DANCE OF HEALTH AND SAFETY

As you welcome your newborn into the world a switch will flip inside of you. One of your biggest missions is going to be keeping your tribe safe and sound. Yep, that's right from day one, it's going to be your superdad duty to ensure your little sidekick is protected from every imaginable bump, scrape, and mishap.

As a greenhorn dad, you're probably feeling a tad overwhelmed. But fear not, my friend, because in this chapter, we're diving headfirst into the thrilling world of family health and protection. Think of it as your crash course in Babyproofing 101, complete with all the insider tips and tricks you need to transform your home into a fortress of safety and love.

Now, let's get real: being a parent is like walking a tightrope without a safety net. One wrong move, and you've got a crying baby on your hands (or worse, a booby trap waiting to happen). But, hey, no pressure! With a little know-how, you'll soon be mastering the delicate dance of parenthood like a seasoned pro.

So, buckle up, dad! From bubble-wrapping your precious cargo to tackling those inevitable boo-boos with finesse, you're about to be equipped with all the tools you need to navigate this wild ride called parenting. Get ready to rock those dad skills and create a haven where your loved ones can thrive. Let's dive in and discover the secrets to becoming your family's ultimate protector!

HOME SAFETY CHECKLIST

I want to give this *"disclaimer"* real quick because so many new dads, jump right in to this feeling this has to be done before the baby arrives. That newborn is not going to be running away from you any time soon, so as you read this, remember you have time! This is advice as we create that safe haven moving forward. *Disclaimer ended!* Creating a comprehensive safety checklist for your home is like giving it a security makeover. Start by surveying every nook and cranny of your house, from the attic to the basement. Look out for common hazards like sharp corners, dangling cords, slippery floors, and unsecured furniture. Make a list of these potential dangers and prioritize them based on severity. Then, tackle each item on your checklist one by one, implementing safety measures such as installing corner guards, securing heavy furniture to the wall, covering electrical outlets, and removing choking hazards. Remember, a thorough safety check can go a long way in preventing accidents and keeping your little one out of harm's way. So, let's be real, kids are going to be kids, and no matter how vigilant you are they will get hurt A LOT, but the efforts we make now can diminish the severity of those dramatic moments. Please note, in the first few weeks to months this isn't a priority as that little one will not be on the move much, but time flies quickly as we all know, and before you know it that poop machine will be on the run... No pun intended!

Childproofing Basics

Alright, let's dive into the basics of childproofing-it's all about making your home safe for your little explorer. Think of it as baby-proofing your place against tiny tornadoes!

First off, put yourself in your baby's shoes (obviously not literally, my big toe is probably bigger). Get down on their level and scope out any trouble spots. Look for things they could grab, chew on, or trip over. You'd be surprised at what catches their eye. You will also realize how big the world is from down there!

Start with the obvious stuff; cover up those electrical outlets, lock away cleaning supplies and medications, and stash away any small objects that could be choking hazards. Basically, if it's small enough to fit in a toilet paper roll, it's a no-go for the baby.

Next, tackle furniture and appliances. Anchor heavy items like bookshelves and TVs to the wall to prevent tipovers. Invest in some baby gates to keep curious kiddos out of off-limits areas. Trust me they like tiny escape artists!

Don't forget about cords and blinds, those dangling temptations can be a strangulation risk. Tie up cords or use cordless blinds to eliminate the danger.

Don't sweat it, we've all been there! Take it one step at a time, starting with the areas your baby will spend the most time in. And remember, no home is ever 100% baby-proof, however, a little effort goes a long way in keeping your little one safe and sound.

Baby Gates and Locks

Installing safety gates and childproof locks is like adding a layer of defense to your home. Baby gates are essential for blocking off stairways, doorways, or other areas that pose a risk to your little crawler. Choose gates that are sturdy, easy to install, and equipped with childproof latches. Similarly, childproof locks help prevent curious hands from accessing cabinets, drawers, and appliances that contain hazardous items or pose safety risks. Invest in quality locks that are durable and reliable, ensuring that they're properly installed and maintained for maximum effectiveness.

Safety gates and baby locks are your secret weapon in the war against toddler exploration. Not that there is anything wrong with your child wanting to explore but it makes it easier to keep them safe if you know where they are. Installing them is pretty straightforward. Most gates come with pressure-mounted or hardware-mounted options.

- Pressure-mounted gates are easy to set up, just adjust the tension to fit snugly between walls or doorframes. They're great for temporary setups or rental homes.
- Hardware-mounted gates, on the other hand, require drilling into the wall or doorframe for a more secure fit. They're ideal for high-traffic areas where you need extra stability.

Now, let's talk about childproof locks. These nifty gadgets come in all shapes and sizes, from simple latches to fancy magnetic locks. They're perfect for keeping little fingers out of cabinets, drawers, and appliances. Installing them is a breeze–most come with adhesive backing or screws for easy attachment. Just make sure to position them out of your child's reach but still accessible for you. I personally got magnetic locks (Amazon is your friend) and they work amazing against little hands (and dogs for that matter)

When it comes to installing safety gates and locks, remember to follow the manufacturer's instructions. Here's a general guide on how to install safety gates and childproof locks:

Safety Gates

1. **Measure the Width:** First, measure how wide the area where you want to install the safety gate is. Make sure to measure at both the top and bottom of the stairs or doorway, as they may not be the same.
2. **Choose the Right Gate:** Select a safety gate that fits the width of your space. There are different types of gates available.
3. **Position the Gate:** Place the gate in the desired location and ensure that it is level. For pressure-mounted gates, adjust the tension to secure it in place. For hardware-mounted gates, use a pencil to mark the locations for drilling.
4. **Drill Pilot Holes:** If you're installing a hardware-mounted gate, use a drill to create pilot holes for the screws. Be sure to follow the manufacturer's instructions for proper placement.
5. **Secure the Gate:** Attach the gate to the wall or doorframe using screws or pressure mounts, depending on the type of the gate. Double-check that the gate is securely in place and can't be easily dislodged.

Childproof Locks

1. **Clean the Surface:** Before installing the childproof lock, clean the surface of the cabinet or drawer where it will be placed. This will ensure better adhesion.
2. **Position the Lock:** Determine the best placement for the childproof lock on the cabinet or drawer, so it's out of reach of your child but still accessible for you.
3. **Peel off the Backing:** If the lock comes with adhesive

backing, peel off the protective covering to expose the adhesive.

4. **Press Firmly:** Press the lock firmly onto the surface, applying pressure for a few seconds to ensure proper adhesion.

5. **Test the Lock:** Once installed, test the lock to make sure it's working correctly. Practice opening and closing it to ensure its secure but easy for you to use.

Double-check that everything is secure before letting your little Houdini loose. And, hey, if you're not the handiest person around, don't worry–there are plenty of tutorials and handyman services out there to lend a helping hand. With these safety measures in place, you can breathe a little easier knowing your home is a safer place for your pint-sized explorer to roam.

Safe Sleep Practices

Next up, make sure your baby has a safe sleeping environment as it's super important. Here's how you can create a cozy and secure sleep setup:

1. **Get a Good Mattress and Sheets:** Having a firm mattress with a fitted sheet your baby's crib or bassinet helps keep them comfy and reduces the risk of accidents.

2. **Skip the Fluffy Stuff:** Keep soft bedding like pillows, blankets, and stuffed animals out of the crib. They might look cute, but they can be risky for your baby's safety.

3. **Back is Best:** Always put your baby to sleep on their back. It's the safest position and helps lower the chance of Sudden Infant Death Syndrome (SIDS).

4. **Keep it Just Right for Goldilocks:** Make sure the room isn't too hot or too cold. Dress your baby in light clothes

and keep the room temperature comfy, around 68 to 72°F (20 to 22°C).

5. **Try a Bedside Crib:** Consider using a bedside crib that attaches to your bed. It's super handy for nighttime feedings and helps you stay close to your baby while they sleep.

When it comes to cribs, I can highly recommend a transitional one. They are definitely the way to go! These awesome cribs grow with your baby, which is super handy. They start as a crib for your newborn, then can be converted into a toddler bed when the time comes, and even into a full-size bed later on. It's like getting three beds in one! You'll save money and space while giving your kid a cozy place to sleep as they grow. It's a win-win.

Baby Monitors

When it comes to keeping an eye (and ear) on your little bundle of joy, baby monitors are a game-changer. Picture this: You're in the kitchen whipping up dinner, and your baby is peacefully napping in their room. With a baby monitor, you can relax knowing that you'll hear the tiniest peep or cry, no matter where you are in the house.

Features to Look For

Think about what matters most to you. Do you want to see your baby as well as hear them? Then look for monitors with video capabilities. Want to chat with your baby from afar? Opt for two-way communication. And don't forget about temperature monitoring to ensure your baby is cozy all night long. Here are some features you can look for in a baby monitor:

1. **Smartphone Compatibility:** Imagine being able to check in on your baby from your smartphone while you're out

running errands or enjoying a night out(anything's possible). With smartphone-compatible monitors, it's totally possible. Get alerts and notifications right on your phone, giving you peace of mind wherever you go.

2. **Range and Signal Quality:** Whether you've got a sprawling mansion or a cozy apartment, you'll want a monitor with a solid range and reliable signal. Look for one that can reach every corner of your home without any pesky interference.

3. **Additional Features:** Night vision for checking in after lights out, soothing lullabies to help your baby drift off to dreamland, and movement sensors for extra peace of mind—these are just a few of the bonus features you might find in a baby monitor.

So, there you have it! Investing in a quality baby monitor means you can rest easy knowing that you'll always be connected to your little one, no matter where life takes you. Honestly if you get a good monitor, it lasts forever and we have used ours in other rooms like our play room just to monitor kids activity.

Emergency Plans

Let's talk emergency plans—not the most exciting topic, but definitely important! Basically, it's all about being prepared for the unexpected. First things first, you gotta think about what kind of emergencies could happen—like fires, natural disasters, or medical situations. Once you've got that figured out, it's time to plan.

1. **Identify Potential Emergencies:** Look at where you live and think about the types of emergencies that could happen. Are you in an area prone to wildfires, floods, hurricanes, tornadoes, earthquakes, or Zombie

Apocalypse? Also, consider medical emergencies or household accidents.

2. **Create a Detailed Plan:** Once you've identified the potential emergencies, sit down with your family, and create a plan for each scenario. Discuss escape routes, safe meeting points, and who's responsible for what. Dad – your responsible for the Zombies!

3. **Assign Roles and Responsibilities:** Make sure everyone in your family knows their role in the emergency plan. Assign tasks like grabbing the emergency kit, shutting off utilities, or assisting younger children or elderly family members.

4. **Establish Meeting Points:** Choose a few meeting points outside of your home where everyone can gather in case of an emergency. These could be nearby landmarks, a neighbor's house, or a designated community center.

5. **Practice, Practice, Practice:** Regularly conduct emergency drills with your family to ensure everyone knows what to do and where to go in case of an emergency. Practice evacuating your home safely and meeting up at the designated meeting points.

6. **Stock up on Emergency Supplies:** Make sure your home is equipped with essential emergency supplies, including a first aid kit, flashlights, batteries, non-perishable food, water, and medications. I'm not asking you to prepare for complete isolation, but remember COVID and nobody had toilet paper..Yikes!

7. **Stay Informed:** Stay updated on local emergency alerts and advisories through news sources, weather apps, or community alert systems. Being informed can help you make quick decisions and take appropriate action when needed.

Remember, the goal of emergency planning is to keep you and your family safe. Taking the time to prepare now can make all the difference when disaster strikes. It might seem like overkill, but trust me, having a solid plan in place saves time, reduces anxiety, and, most importantly, ensures the welfare of your family. At the end of the day, isn't that what the job of being the best Dad is all about?

NUTRITION AND WELLNESS: HEALTHY HABITS

While on the topic of health and planning, one big question dads ask is when and how to introduce their baby to solid foods.

Introducing solid foods to your baby is an exciting milestone, but it's essential to wait until they're developmentally ready. Typically, most babies are ready to start solids around six months of age. However, every baby is different, so it's crucial to watch for signs of readiness, such as:

1. **Head Control:** Your baby should be able to sit up with support and hold their head steady.
2. **Loss of Tongue Thrust Reflex:** Babies have a natural reflex that pushes food out of their mouths with their tongues. When they're ready for solids, this reflex diminishes.
3. **Increased Appetite:** If your baby seems interested in what you're eating and seems unsatisfied with just breast milk or formula, it may be a sign that they're ready to try solids.
4. **Ability to Chew or Gnaw:** Your baby may start showing an interest in chewing on toys or other objects, indicating they're developing the necessary oral motor skills for eating solid foods.

Once you notice these signs of readiness, you can begin introducing solids gradually, starting with simple purees or soft, mashed foods.

1. **Take it Slow:** Yep, slow, and steady wins the race here. Begin with simple purees like mashed bananas or sweet potatoes. Then gradually introduce new foods one at a time. This helps you keep track of how your baby reacts to each new taste and texture.

2. **Watch for Allergies:** Allergies are no joke, especially when it comes to your little one. Keep an eagle eye out for any signs of allergic reactions, like rashes, hives, vomiting, or difficulty breathing. Common allergens to be cautious of include nuts, dairy, eggs, and shellfish.

3. **Consult With Your Doc:** When in doubt, don't hesitate to reach out to your pediatrician. They're the experts and can offer guidance tailored to your baby's needs. If you're unsure about a particular food or concerned about potential allergies, it's always best to get their input.

Remember, every baby is different, so go at your own pace and trust your instincts. Before you know it, your little one will be exploring a whole world of flavors and textures. A great hack from experienced dads–several baby food makers will steam and puree your food. A great trick is to just add some of the food you're already preparing for yourself or your family and get it prepped for the little one. This way you don't have to go out of your way and the baby has a fresh healthier food than some of those off-the-shelf stuff. Also, A TON cheaper. You can also get some silicone ice trays and puree food like sweet potatoes or other baby favorites and put in the trays to freeze. This is a huge timesaver and a sweet way to have a supply in a hurry with a quick microwave. This has saved me quite a bit of money and, honestly, I felt better knowing exactly what my baby was eating.

Family Mealtime

Family meals are more than just an opportunity to refuel–they're a chance to connect and bond with your loved ones. So, when it's time to gather around the table, make it a moment to cherish. Set aside some dedicated time each day to sit down together, share stories, and catch up on everyone's day. Whether it's breakfast, lunch, or dinner, make it a ritual to come together and enjoy each other's company. I know I'm making this statement prematurely, but the impact this can make long term is worth putting the bug in your ear now.

And let's not forget about the food itself! We all have our unique tastes and dietary needs, whether it's allergies, intolerances, or simply personal preferences. But that doesn't mean we can't all enjoy a delicious meal together. Get creative in the kitchen and explore new recipes that cater to everyone's needs. Whether it's finding dairy-free alternatives, gluten-free options, or simply swapping ingredients to accommodate picky eaters, there's always a way to ensure everyone has something tasty on their plate.

At the end of the day, it's all about keeping the love and laughter alive around the dinner table. So, embrace the quirks, celebrate the differences, and enjoy the simple pleasure of sharing a meal with the ones you love. After all, good food and good company are the recipe for a happy and healthy family life!

Physical Activity and Exercise

Physical activity is key to keeping the whole family healthy and happy. It's not just about hitting the gym–it's about finding fun ways to move together and stay active in your daily lives.

For the little ones, it's all about playtime! Encourage activities like tummy time, crawling, and supervised floor play to help them develop their motor skills and stay active. As they grow, make sure they have plenty of opportunities for active play and exploration.

As for the adults and older kids, aim for at least 60 minutes of moderate to vigorous physical activity each day. Whether it's walking, biking, swimming, or playing sports, find activities that you enjoy and make them a regular part of your routine.

But why stop there? Take your workouts outside and explore the great outdoors as a family. Plan outings to local parks, nature trails, or playgrounds for some fresh air and adventure. Whether you're hiking, biking, or just enjoying a picnic, outdoor activities are a great way to bond as a family while staying active. So many people feel that since they have an infant, they can't do these things..... hosh posh! Getting your child acclimated to these activities makes it a part of their normal routine, and creates an amazing healthy lifestyle blueprint for their future.

And don't forget about routine health check-ups! Regular visits to your pediatrician or family doctor are crucial for monitoring your family's health and catching any potential issues early on. So, schedule those appointments, stay proactive about preventive care, and keep your family happy, healthy, and active for years to come!

Emergency Preparedness

I know I have said this before, but I have to say it again, emergencies can happen, and more often than not when you least expect them. And I can't stress it enough that being prepared can and will make all the difference. First things first, stock up on first aid essentials. Put together a handy first aid kit with all the basics—bandages, antiseptic wipes, gauze pads, adhesive tape, scissors, tweezers, and pain relievers. Also, invest in a digital ear thermometer to check the temperature of your baby. Oh, they still sell those fun thermometers that go elsewhere, but the ear thermometer is easier to use, less abrasive, and makes checking for a fever quick and easy. They also have forehead surface thermometers, but the cheaper ones do not work the best in my experience. If you want to invest in a more medical hospital grade, then these are even easier. Get familiar with each item in your kit and practice using them so you'll be ready to spring into action when needed. I can clean, sterilize and apply a Band-Aid in under 2 minutes – time me!

Next up, consider getting CPR training. CPR (Cardiopulmonary Resuscitation) can be a lifesaver in critical situations, especially for infants and children. Look into courses offered by organizations like the Red Cross, where you'll learn essential lifesaving skills, including CPR techniques tailored for different age groups. With the right training, you'll feel confident and equipped to respond effectively during emergencies.

Choking is a scary situation, especially for little ones who love exploring with their mouths. Learn how to recognize the signs of choking and how to perform the Heimlich maneuver or back blows to dislodge an obstructed airway. Do you know that it's different for infants? If you don't, then get to a class! Keep small objects and foods that could pose choking hazards out of reach, and always keep a close eye on young children during mealtime and play.

Burns and scalds can happen in the blink of an eye, but knowing how to treat them promptly can help minimize pain and prevent further damage. Learn basic first aid techniques for treating burns, like cooling the affected area with running water and covering it with a clean cloth. Take precautions to prevent burns and scalds by adjusting water heater temperatures, using stove guards, and keeping hot liquids out of reach of children.

Lastly, safeguard your home against poisoning hazards. Keep household chemicals, medications, and other toxic substances out of reach and locked away. Use childproof locks on cabinets containing hazardous items, and make sure products are stored in their original containers with child-resistant caps. Educate your family, including older kids, about the dangers of ingesting poisonous substances and what to do in case of accidental ingestion. If you always keep the same cleaning materials around, you can "Google search" Material Safety Data Sheets for (insert chemical name) and it will give you everything you need to do if in your eyes, on skin, or ingested, along with more information than you'll never care to know. With these precautions in place, you'll be better prepared to handle emergencies and keep your loved ones safe.

Safety on the Go

Whether you're running errands or embarking on a family road trip, safety on the go is paramount. Here is what you should keep an eye on:

Car Seat Safety

Installing and using car seats properly is non-negotiable when it comes to protecting your little ones in the car. Make sure you read the instructions carefully and install the seat according to the manufacturer's guidelines as we've discussed earlier in the book. Remember, newborns should ride in rear-facing seats, and as they grow, they'll move up to forward-facing seats and then booster seats. Keep an eye on your car seat for any signs of wear and tear and replace it if needed to keep your kiddos safe.

Seatbelt and Booster Seat Guidelines

As your children outgrow car seats, it's time to transition them to booster seats and eventually just use seat belts. Follow the recommended guidelines based on their age, weight, and height. Teach them the importance of buckling up properly, and make sure you're setting a good example by wearing your seat belt every time you hit the road.

Travel Safety

Whether you're traveling by car, plane, or any other mode of transportation, there are a few things you need to do to keep your family safe. If you're staying in a hotel or vacation rental, grab a few childproof locks from home and put them on doors and windows to keep curious kiddos safe. Keep all your important documents, medications, and emergency contact info handy while traveling, and have a plan in place for any unexpected situations that might arise.

As a first-time dad, your top priority is keeping your family safe and sound. It's not just about meeting their physical needs, but also creating a loving and secure environment where they can thrive. When you are promoting healthy habits, implementing safety measures, and preparing for emergencies, you're showing your loved ones just how much you care.

Your commitment to your family's well-being is an ongoing journey filled with ups and downs. Whether you're stocking up a first aid kit or making sure the car seat is installed just right, every little thing you do to keep them safe is a reflection of your love and dedication as a parent.

So, keep prioritizing their health and safety, knowing that your unwavering love and care are the greatest gifts you can give them.

With you by their side, they'll be ready to take on whatever adventures life throws their way.

MAKE A DIFFERENCE WITH YOUR REVIEW
UNLOCK THE POWER OF FATHERHOOD

When you teach a man to father, you benefit his children for a lifetime.

ADAPTED FROM THE OLD SAYING "GIVE A
MAN A FISH"

Helping out can make you feel good inside, like when you share your toys or help a friend. Imagine feeling that happy just by writing a few words to help other dads learn how to be great fathers.

Do you remember how it felt when you first learned you were going to be a dad? Maybe you were excited, or maybe you were a bit scared, just like I was. Now think about all the new dads who are feeling that way right now. They need a friend to guide them, and that friend could be you!

Our book, *"Dads-to-Be: First-Time Fathers Guide"*, is here to help every dad be the hero his kids think he is. But we can only reach more dads if people know about our book. And that's where you come in!

Most people pick a book based on what others say about it. So, I have a big favor to ask for all those new dads out there:

Would you please write a review for this book?

It won't cost you a penny, and it'll take less than a minute, but your words could help:

- One more dad feel ready for his new baby.

- One more family grow stronger together.

- One more worker balance his job and home life better.

- One more person change their life in ways they never imagined.

- One more dream of a happy family come true.

All you have to do to spread a little kindness is leave a review by scanning the QR code below:

If you enjoy helping others, even if you don't see their smiles, then you're awesome, and I'm glad you're here! Welcome to the club. You're one of us now.

I'm excited to help you master fatherhood more easily and quickly than you thought possible. You're going to love the tips and tricks I've packed into this book.

Thank you from the bottom of my heart. Now, let's get back to learning how to be the best dad ever.

- Your buddy and guide, D.MoSon

P.S. - Did you know? When you help someone, it makes you a superhero in their eyes (or at least pretty darn cool). If you think this book can help another dad, why not share it with him? It's a great way to spread the joy of fatherhood!

CHAPTER 5

BABY'S FIRST YEAR

FROM COOING CUTIE TO MINIATURE MISCHIEF MAKER, ALL THE MILESTONES AND CHALLENGES IN BETWEEN

As you watch your little one, so much will happen that first year. Every week seems to be something new they can do, and a milestone that has been reached. From those delicate first days, to the whirlwind of toddlerhood, every step has been a mix of awe and growth. As a rookie dad, celebrating this milestone isn't just about throwing a birthday bash–it's about acknowledging the incredible journey you and your child will take together.

Let me tell you a funny story about Jay, a dad of four, reflecting on his adventures with his boys. There was this one time when he was rushing to get out the door and had to quickly change his son Jacob's diaper. So, he plopped Jacob on the kitchen table for a lightning-fast diaper swap. But here's the kicker: as soon as the diaper came off, Jacob decided it was the perfect moment for a little pee-pee parade. With unbelievable precision, he managed to douse Jay's unsuspecting coffee cup with a graceful arc of liquid gold. Not a drop touched Jacob, but Jay's coffee cup? Let's just say it retired early that day. Lesson learned? Never underestimate a newborn's aim, and always watch out for surprise sprinkles!

As you toast your child's first birthday, take a moment to savor the beautiful chaos and unexpected hijinks that come with being a parent. From diaper dilemmas to spontaneous escapades, each moment is a testament to the laughter and resilience that define fatherhood. So, here's to your little mischief-maker and many more years of love, laughter, and unforgettable adventures together!

GIGGLES, GROUCHES, AND GRINS-SURVIVING THE MERRY-GO-ROUND OF EMOTIONS

There are going to be many moments and as the old man told you a million times: "Enjoy it now, as it goes by fast." Ah, the wisdom of the old-timers! They've seen it all, haven't they? And they're not shy about reminding us to savor every moment because, believe me, it flies by faster than you can say "diaper change."

Newborn Bliss

Newborn bliss–those precious, unforgettable moments that tug at the heartstrings and etch themselves into your memory forever. Picture it: you're cradling your tiny newborn in your arms for the very first time. The weight of their little body, the softness of their skin, the delicate scent that envelops you–it's a sensory overload like no other.

As you gaze down at their tiny face, a wave of emotions washes over you. There's the overwhelming love that fills your heart to the brim, so intense it's almost palpable. You find yourself marveling at the miracle of life, at this tiny human being that you helped bring into the world. It's a feeling of awe and wonder unlike anything you've ever experienced before.

But amidst the joy and wonder, there's also a hint of disbelief–a pinch of "holy moly, I'm a parent!" It's a surreal moment, realizing that you're now responsible for this precious little life, entrusted with their care and well-being. And yet, despite the enormity of the task ahead, there's a sense of peace and contentment that settles over you, knowing that you're exactly where you're meant to be.

In those first moments of newborn bliss, time seems to stand still as you drink in every detail of your baby's tiny features–the curve of their cheeks, the flutter of their eyelashes, the sweet sound of their soft, contented sighs. It's a moment of pure, unadulterated joy, a glimpse into a love so fierce and unconditional that it takes your breath away.

So close your eyes, dear parent, and let yourself be transported back to that magical moment of newborn bliss. Let the memories wash over you like a warm embrace, filling you with gratitude for the precious gift of parenthood and the boundless love that comes with it.

Sleepless Nights

Sleepless nights–the rite of passage for every new parent, where exhaustion becomes the new normal and coffee becomes your best friend. Picture this: it's the dead of night, and you find yourself stumbling through the dimly lit hallways, bleary-eyed and delirious, in a desperate attempt to soothe your fussy little one back to sleep. Sound familiar? Welcome to the club, my sleep-deprived friend.

But, hey, let's not dwell on the negatives. Sure, the lack of sleep can leave you feeling like a walking zombie, but there's a certain camaraderie to be found in those wee hours of the morning. Like the time you accidentally put the diaper on backward and didn't realize it until halfway through the change–oops! Or how about the moment you discovered your hidden talent for changing a diaper in record time, all while half-asleep and barely coherent? Who knew sleep deprivation could bring out your inner superhero?

And let's not forget the unexpected moments of hilarity that can only happen in the dead of night. Like that time your baby let out the loudest, most epic burp you've ever heard, or when they pulled off the most impressive karate kick mid-diaper change. It's moments like these that remind you that even amid exhaustion, there's still plenty of laughter to be found.

So, here's to the sleepless nights, dear parent, and the countless adventures they bring. Embrace the chaos, cherish the moments of unexpected joy, and remember that this too shall pass. And when all else fails, just pour yourself another cup of coffee and know that you're not alone in this wild and wonderful journey called parenthood.

First Smiles and Laughs

The magic of first smiles and laughs—those precious milestones that make all the sleepless nights and diaper disasters fade into the background. Imagine this: you're cradling your little one in your arms, their eyes lighting up with sheer delight as they gaze up at you. And then it happens—the corners of their mouth twitch into the most adorable grin, and your heart feels like it's about to burst with love.

It's a moment of pure magic, like a beam of sunlight breaking through the clouds on a stormy day. Suddenly, all the exhaustion and chaos of parenthood seem to melt away, replaced by an overwhelming sense of joy and wonder. You find yourself grinning right back at your baby, feeling like the luckiest person in the world to witness such a precious sight.

But wait, it gets even better. Just when you think your heart can't possibly hold any more love, your baby lets out their first giggle–a sound so sweet and infectious, it's like music to your ears. And at that moment, you realize that all the sleepless nights, the endless feedings, and the countless diaper changes were leading up to this–the sound of your baby's laughter filling your home with happiness and laughter.

Enjoy these moments, my friend, for they're the ones that make every challenge of parenthood totally worth it. Take a mental snapshot of that toothless grin and that melodic giggle and hold it tight. Because before you know it, your little one will be all grown up, and these precious moments will become cherished memories to look back on with a smile.

Navigating Parenthood Challenges

We've covered a lot of ground so far and we're not done yet. It's time to take a moment and turn our attention to our partners. The ones without whom all the joys of being a parent would not be possible. After giving birth, her body has been through the wringer–think of it like being tackled by a linebacker, NFL-style. So, it's no surprise that she might need some extra TLC during those first few weeks.

You might find her spending a lot of time on the couch, recovering from the physical toll of childbirth, and adjusting to her new role as a mom. It's essential to be there for her, whether it's fetching snacks, changing diapers, or simply offering a listening ear and a hug.

But postpartum adjustments aren't just physical–they're emotional too. Your partner may experience a bunch of different emotions, from overwhelming joy to moments of doubt and anxiety. Be patient, be understanding, and most importantly, be there for her every step of the way.

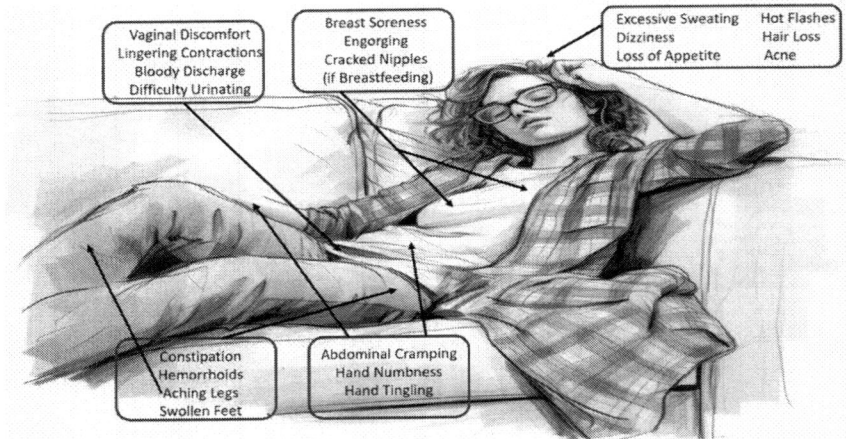

It's important to balance responsibilities. With a new baby in the mix, it's more important than ever to divide and conquer when it comes to household duties. Sit down together and discuss who will take on what tasks, whether it's diaper duty, meal prep, or laundry.

But here's the thing—it's not just about divvying up chores. It's also about making sure both partners have time for self-care. Parenthood can be all-consuming, but it's crucial to carve out time for yourselves, whether it's a solo trip to the gym, a bubble bath, or a Netflix binge session.

Remember, you're a team, and navigating parenthood together means supporting each other through the ups and downs. So, be there for your partner, communicate openly and honestly, and above all, cherish these moments together as you embark on this incredible journey as your baby grows.

Speaking of a growing baby. Let's dive into some key aspects of your baby's development:

1. **Coping With Crying:** When your little one just won't stop crying, it can be challenging to know what to do. That's where Dr. Harvey Karp's "Five S's" come in handy. These techniques—swaddling, side/stomach position, shushing, swinging, and sucking—can help soothe your baby and provide comfort during those fussy moments. Swaddle—wrap up your little burrito to keep their arms in tight. This helps any of those flailing arms from scratching as well as reduces the startle reflex. Side/Stomach position—hold your baby on their stomach or side or even over your shoulder. However, it's very important to note that you can hold babies on their side or stomach, but it is NOT safe to place a baby on the side or stomach to sleep. The back is the only safe position for sleeping. Shushing—make a "shhhh" sound or possibly use a white noise machine. Swinging—swing or jiggle in fast tiny (like 1 inch) movements while supporting their head and neck. Sucking—sucking on a pacifier, bottle or breast helps soothe the baby.

2. **Baby's Health and Wellness:** Keeping your baby healthy and happy is a top priority. Regular well-baby check-ups with your pediatrician are essential for monitoring your baby's growth and development, receiving vaccinations, and addressing any concerns you may have about their health.

3. **Rolling Over and Sitting Up:** Celebrate each of your baby's milestones, from rolling over to sitting up independently. These physical achievements are signs of your baby's growing strength and coordination. Encourage their development by providing plenty of supervised

tummy time and engaging in activities that support their motor skills.

4. **Crawling and First Steps:** Get ready to be amazed as your little one begins to explore the world on all fours and eventually takes their first steps. Celebrate these milestones and provide a safe environment for your baby to practice their newfound mobility. Keep an eye out for potential hazards and offer plenty of encouragement and support as they navigate this exciting stage of development. This is when all those safety guards we spoke about prior need to go in to full affect.

5. **First Words:** Hearing your baby's first words is a momentous occasion. Encourage language development by talking and reading to your baby from an early age. Respond to their babbling with enthusiasm and engage in conversations to help them learn and communicate. Just for the record "Dadda" is easier to say, so don't celebrate in front of your partner too long, but maybe have your dance moves ready!

6. **Teething Troubles:** Teething can be a challenging time for both babies and parents. Look out for signs of teething, such as excessive drooling, irritability, and chewing on objects. Provide relief by offering teething toys, chilled washcloths, or gentle massages to soothe sore gums. Over-the-counter pain relievers may also help alleviate discomfort but be sure to consult with your pediatrician before giving any medication to your baby.

By staying informed and proactive about your baby's development and well-being, you can support their growth and provide a nurturing environment for them to thrive. Enjoy each moment of this incredible journey as you witness your baby's milestones and cherish the precious memories along the way.

As your baby grows, you'll notice them becoming more independent, exploring their surroundings, and asserting their preferences. While fostering independence is important for their development, it's equally crucial to nurture a secure attachment between you and your baby.

1. **Encourage exploration:** Provide a safe and stimulating environment for your baby to explore independently. Offer age-appropriate toys and activities that encourage curiosity and discovery. Allow them to move freely and explore their surroundings under your supervision.
2. **Offer support and encouragement:** As your baby attempts to practice new skills, such as crawling, standing, or feeding themselves, offer gentle guidance and encouragement. Celebrate their achievements, no matter how small, to boost their confidence and sense of accomplishment.
3. **Respect their preferences:** As your baby develops their own likes and dislikes, respect their preferences and autonomy. Offer choices when appropriate and allow them to make decisions, such as selecting toys or foods. This helps them develop a sense of independence and autonomy.
4. **Maintain a secure bond:** A secure and loving connection forms the foundation for healthy emotional development and relationships. Create bonding opportunities through physical touch, eye contact, and responsive caregiving. Respond promptly to your baby's cues for comfort and reassurance, whether they're hungry, tired, or in need of affection.
5. **Foster emotional connection:** Spend quality time bonding with your baby through activities like cuddling, playing, and reading together. Engage in interactions that

promote emotional connection and communication. Be attuned to your baby's emotions and provide comfort and support during times of distress.

6. **Create routines and rituals:** Establishing predictable routines and rituals can provide a sense of security and stability for your baby. Consistent daily routines, such as bedtime rituals or mealtime routines, help your baby feel safe and understand what to expect in their environment.

By promoting your child's independence with the nurturing of a deep parent-child connection, you can support your baby's development and lay the groundwork for healthy relationships and emotional well-being throughout their life.

LOOKING AHEAD

As your child's first birthday approaches, it's a momentous occasion that marks not only the passage of time but also the beginning of an incredible journey ahead. Reflecting on the past year, you may feel a mix of emotions—pride in your parenting accomplishments, nostalgia for the fleeting moments, and excitement for the adventures yet to come.

Brace yourself for the ups and downs of toddlerhood, known affectionately as the "terrible twos." This stage is characterized by newfound independence, strong emotions, and boundary-pushing behavior. While it may present challenges, it's also a time of immense growth and discovery for your child.

Build a strong foundation of family rituals and traditions that will create lasting memories you can come back to when your child is all grown up. Whether it's a weekly movie night, holiday traditions, or annual outings, these shared experiences strengthen family bonds and provide a sense of belonging for everyone.

Amid busy schedules and everyday distractions, make a conscious effort to be fully present and engaged in your child's life. Cherish the simple moments, like bedtime stories and playtime adventures, and prioritize quality time together. Your presence and involvement are invaluable gifts to your child.

Remember this is a never-ending journey, so tackle it head-on and be ready to meet new opportunities for growth, learning, and connection. Embrace the challenges and joys that lie ahead, knowing that your love and support are the guiding forces that will shape your child's future.

As you celebrate your child's first birthday(smash cake is the best pictures), take a moment to savor the milestones and memories of the past year. From the sleepless nights to the first smiles and everything in between, each moment has contributed to the beautiful tapestry of your journey as a father. And remember, this is just the beginning of a lifetime of love, laughter, and adventure as you continue to write the story of fatherhood.

CHAPTER 6
NAVIGATING PARENTHOOD WITH A PARTNER

KEEPING THE FLAME ALIVE

P arenthood is undoubtedly an amazing adventure, but let's face it, it can throw some curveballs when it comes to keeping the romance alive in your relationship. Parenthood has a way of reshaping your priorities like nothing else. Suddenly, the late nights out and spontaneous adventures take a backseat to diaper changes and bedtime stories. It's a shift that can catch you off guard, but Derris, a seasoned father of two, offers sage advice: be patient. Adding a child to the mix brings a new level of complexity to your relationship, but it also brings excitement and growth. Or as Nick, another new dad, admits that becoming a father was not the easiest transition for him and his partner Jamie. "We were a young couple and weren't married yet. When we had our son, Chase, I really did not know how we were going to pull this parenting thing off, as Jamie and I had only dated for 2 months before she announced our surprise pregnancy. Honestly, we were still getting to get to know each other better while we were new parents. It was A LOT of talking, frustrations, and debates the first few months.

Thankfully our church was the one that slapped me out of my funk and helped us realize we were a team and needed to act as one. We got more involved in the church activities, engaged with other young couples who were also attending every Sunday, and come to find out I was pretty darn lucky to have Jamie in my life. She has motivated me to be a better man, husband, and father, and I pray I have been able to provide her with the same support. If it wasn't for our church family, I would not have my family with Jamie and our three amazing, rambunctious monsters that have become my life! So, embrace the changes, look forward to the next phase of life, and remember to give yourselves grace as you navigate this journey together.

Rediscovering the importance of physical affection and intimacy in your relationship is like rediscovering a hidden treasure. It's a vital component that strengthens the bond between partners, but it's essential to recognize that each person has their own timeline for readiness (especially for women after pregnancy!). Communication and mutual respect play crucial roles here. By openly discussing your needs and desires with your partner, you can ensure that you're both on the same page and that intimacy unfolds naturally and comfortably.

Effective communication becomes even more critical as you embark on the challenges of parenthood. Raising a kid can be overwhelming at times but having open and honest communication with your partner can help alleviate stress and strengthen your connection. By expressing your thoughts, concerns, and feelings openly, you can work together as a team to overcome obstacles and celebrate successes.

Working as a united front in parenting decisions and responsibilities is key to maintaining harmony in your relationship. When you establish clear strategies and goals together, you can strengthen your bond as a couple and as parents. When both are involved in decision-making and equally share responsibilities, it fosters a sense of teamwork.

Recognizing and appreciating each other's contributions to the family is vital for nurturing a strong and healthy relationship. Whether it's providing emotional support, handling household chores, or nurturing the baby, acknowledging, and valuing each other's efforts creates a sense of partnership and mutual admiration.

Carving out time for romantic getaways and special moments together is essential for keeping the spark alive in your relationship amidst the demands of parenthood. Date nights and quality time allow you to reconnect with your partner on a deeper level, creating cherished memories that strengthen your bond. When you spend alone time with your partner, you can nurture your connection and keep the romance alive, even during busy schedules and responsibilities.

REKINDLING THE FLAME: NOTE, IT'S NOT A STOPWATCH!

Parenthood can definitely put a strain on romantic relationships, but fear not! With a little intentional effort, you can keep the flame of love burning bright for years to come.

Surprising your partner with thoughtful gestures is like adding fuel to the fire of romance. Whether it's leaving love notes around the house, picking up their favorite treat, or simply doing something sweet for no reason at all–these little acts of kindness can reignite the spark in your relationship and remind your partner just how much they mean to you.

Embrace the spontaneity of life and take advantage of unexpected opportunities to create romantic moments. Whether it's a spontaneous picnic in the park, a surprise dinner date at home, or even just stealing a quiet moment together during a hectic day, embracing spontaneity adds excitement and freshness to your relationship.

Keep things exciting by trying out new activities and adventures together as a family. Whether it's exploring a new hiking trail, checking out a new restaurant, or even just trying out a new recipe together at home, shared experiences strengthen your bond and create memories that last a lifetime.

Never underestimate the power of physical closeness and affectionate gestures. Hugs, kisses, cuddles, and gentle touches can speak volumes and reaffirm your love and connection, even when both of you are dead tired and the only thing you need is to hit the pillow.

Communication is key, so practice active listening when your partner speaks. Show genuine interest and attentiveness, and make sure they feel heard and valued. This kind of communication fosters understanding and emotional intimacy, which are essential for a healthy and thriving relationship.

Finally, show empathy and understanding towards your partner, especially during challenging times. Parenthood can be tough. There will inevitably be ups and downs along the way. Being there for each other with compassion and support strengthens your bond and deepens your connection, ensuring that your flame of love continues to burn bright, no matter what life throws your way.

FACING PARENTHOOD CHALLENGES TOGETHER

Parenthood is a whirlwind of emotions, blending moments of pure joy with bouts of stress and uncertainty. However, facing these challenges together as a team will ease the hardship of parenting and can deepen the bond between you and your partner.

Don't just be there when it's all good but be there during the tough moments as well. As it's those difficult times that truly bring you closer together. As you parent, show each other support by listening and giving a comforting hug. Support and understanding can go a long way in strengthening your relationship.

It's crucial to carve out some time away from parenting duties to recharge and rejuvenate. By coordinating breaks and allowing each other the opportunity to unwind, you can prevent burnout and maintain a sense of balance in your lives.

Respecting each other's need for personal space and self-care is also essential. Recognize that everyone requires moments of solitude to decompress and recharge and be mindful of honoring your partner's downtime.

If you find yourselves grappling with certain issues or the same conflicts keep popping up, sit down and talk about it. But don't just talk and respond, really listen to what the other is saying and try to understand their point of view. If all else fails, don't hesitate to seek couples' counseling or therapy. Asking for help can provide valuable insights and strategies for navigating challenges and maintaining a healthier, more resilient relationship.

Building a robust support network of friends and family is equally important. Surround yourselves with individuals who can offer guidance, advice, and encouragement during difficult times, providing a sense of comfort and reassurance.

Furthermore, don't forget to uplift and encourage each other in pursuing personal and career goals. By championing each other's aspirations, you not only foster individual growth but also strengthen the foundation of your partnership.

Ultimately, remember that personal growth is a journey you embark on together. Embrace the notion that evolving as individuals enriches your relationship, allowing you to grow and flourish together amidst the ever-changing landscape of parenthood.

Parenthood is a journey that tests your love while also providing opportunities to strengthen it. When you actively nurture your relationship and do your best to keep the flames of intimacy alive, you're investing in the health and bright future of your family.

Tackling parenting challenges together will help to cultivate a love that not only withstands but flourishes amidst the joyful chaos of raising children. Your partnership forms the very foundation of your family, so it's worth dedicating time, effort, and affection to fortify its enduring strength and happiness.

But how do you keep the flame alive, raise kids, and work on your career? Let's explore some options in the next chapter!

CHAPTER 7

3 RINGED CIRCUS

BALANCING WORK, FAMILY, AND SELF

S triking the right balance between work, family, and personal well-being can feel like juggling three rings in a circus but instead of rings in chainsaws the ones you have are on fire. Okay, that is a little too dramatic, but it can become hectic, and before you know it, you burn out. Poof. you start feeling crazy and anxious. However, there is always a solution to any problem.

In this chapter, we'll explore strategies to manage each aspect of your life effectively, ensuring that none gets neglected while still making time for the others (and self!).

- **Work:** Your career is an integral part of your life, but maintaining boundaries is essential to prevent it from overshadowing other aspects. Setting realistic goals, prioritizing tasks, and delegating responsibilities can help you stay focused and productive while maintaining a healthy work-life balance.
- **Family:** Nurturing your family relationships requires time, attention, and effort. Make it a priority to carve out quality time for your loved ones, whether it's through family

dinners, weekend outings, or bedtime stories. Effective communication, active listening, and a supportive environment are key to building strong familial bonds.

- **Self-care:** Taking care of yourself is crucial for your overall well-being and ability to handle life's challenges. Make self-care a non-negotiable part of your routine by prioritizing activities that replenish your physical, mental, and emotional health. This can be activities like hobbies, relaxation techniques, or simply taking moments for solitude and reflection (you know, chill in your mancave while tinkering with something).

Finding balance among these three rings of life is tricky, but flexibility, adaptability, and sometimes, a bit of trial and error you can get yourself a perfect daily routine that will keep you sane and productive. And if you feel you can't do it or don't know, how remember that it's okay to ask for help. Seek support from loved ones, and adjust your priorities as needed. By nurturing each part of your life while making time for others, you can create a harmonious and fulfilling lifestyle for yourself and your family. Everything is possible with a cool head and proper planning.

EXCELLING AT WORK AND FATHERHOOD

So, let's talk about adjusting your work schedule when you've got a new bundle of joy in the house. It's a real balancing act, right? You've gotta figure out how to juggle your work duties while still being there for your family, especially with a new baby and sleep deprivation in the mix. The first step is parental leave.

Having a chat with your boss about parental leave and looking into flexible work options can really shake things up. Whether it means snagging some time off to hang with your little one or tweaking your work hours to suit your family's schedule, it's all about finding that sweet spot where you can crush it at work and be a super dad at home too.

Navigating Career Changes

When you're mulling over a career move, it's essential to think about how it'll shake things up at home. A new gig might mean longer hours or more time on the road, which could affect your fam-bam time. Having some heart-to-hearts with your partner about how these changes will play out in family land is key. You wanna make sure everyone's on the same page and that your decisions line up with your family goals.

And let's not forget the rollercoaster of emotions that often comes with switching things up career-wise. Having your squad–whether it's your crew, your fam, or some wise mentors–in your corner can be a game-changer. Getting advice from folks who've been there and done that can help calm those nerves and give you some solid insights into what's ahead.

Oh, and speaking of what's ahead, don't forget to think about the green stuff. Yeah, I'm talkin' about money. When you're considering a new job or career path, carefully check the financial side of things. Will it help you reach your family's financial goals? What about benefits and opportunities for growth? Crunching those numbers and weighing the pros and cons will help you decide that's not just good for your career but also for your loved ones. Carefully check the financial side of things. What about benefits and opportunities for growth? Crunching those numbers and weighing advantages and disadvantages will help you make a decision that's not just good for your career but also for your homies.

At the end of the day, it's all about keeping the lines of communication open with your partner and making choices that support both your professional dreams and your role as an awesome dad.

Career Ambitions vs. Parenthood

Finding that sweet spot between chasing your career dreams and being there for your kiddos is like doing a delicate dance routine. It takes some serious self-reflection, a good dose of thinking things through, and a solid grasp on what matters to you in life. Like the choice Doug had to make.

Doug vividly remembers facing the choice between working for a large corporation offering lucrative benefits that came with long hours but with substantial pay, and even a free leased BMW or versus a smaller company with fewer financial perks, a more active role in the brands development but also a strong and more flexible commitment to family. Fast forward 14 years, when he thinks back and looks at everything he has and knows now, the choice he made was right. He chose the smaller company with less money that provided him with the ability to manage the commitment to the family and work. The smaller company also offered more support of an individual vs being a number in a larger corporation and having little leeway. 14 years later and four more children proved that he money and free BMWs are not necessarily the best investment for his career. Today, Doug would not change a thing in the life he created by following his heart and what was important for him. He is very confident that he made the right choice when he prioritized his family over job benefits. When you are faced with challenges and don't know how to proceed, go over the steps listed below to find what's really important to you:

- **Reflect on Your Values:**

Pause for a moment and dig deep into your values. Think about what really lights you up in your career and what fills your heart at home with your family. A wise man once stated to "Enjoy what you do and you'll never work a day of your life". Understanding your core values will give you a solid base for making decisions that ring true to who you are.

- **Reassess Your Goals:**

Let's take a step back and look at your goals. Parenthood has a way of reshaping our priorities, so it's a good time to reassess what you want out of your career and family life. Take a moment to ponder if your current goals still align with your new role as a parent. It might mean tweaking your career path, finding a better balance between work and family, or redefining what success means to you.

- **Set Realistic Expectations:**

Let's be real here–finding the perfect balance between work and family life can be tough. It's important to have realistic expectations that are actually realistic, rather than trying to live up to some impossible standards. Understand that this balance might change over time as your family grows and evolves, and that's totally okay. Stay flexible and focus on what works best for you at the moment. Understand the reality and set realistic expectations for what you want to achieve.

- **Prioritize Your Time:**

Time–probably the most precious thing we've got in this crazy balancing act of work and family life. It's all about setting priorities, drawing clear lines, and being intentional about how you spend your time. Sometimes work's gonna take the front seat, and that's okay, but it's equally important to carve out those sacred moments for your family too. It's like juggling–knowing when to catch that work ball and when to catch that family ball, without dropping either. This is where a family calendar also comes in handy. With technology today, whether it's your phone calendar with specific groups invited/shared or the hundreds of apps out there; find something that works well between you, your partner and I suggest any other "support staff" that helps with your family, as we know it takes a village to raise a child successfully.

- **Open Communication with Your Partner:**

Keep those lines of communication wide open with your partner. tête-à-tête but with a dash of logistics thrown in. Share your career dreams, talk about the crazy workload, and figure out how it all fits into your family puzzle. When you're both on the same page, making decisions becomes a team effort, and everyone's needs get a fair shake. And if you ever feel you're in a bind, don't hesitate to seek support from mentors, colleagues, or friends who have successfully navigated the challenges of balancing career ambitions with parenthood. Learning from others' experiences can provide valuable insights and practical strategies for finding equilibrium. Let them know what you want to achieve and how you can balance your work with family obligations. Being honest and flexible will enable you to satisfy your ambitions and execute your duties as a father.

Recognize that life is dynamic, and your career and family priorities will evolve and change over time. Embrace flexibility and be open to adjusting your plans as needed. This adaptability allows you to navigate the changing landscape of both your professional and personal life and you need to tailor things to meet your needs and wants.

Ultimately, finding the right balance between career ambitions and parenthood is a unique journey for everyone. Stay true to your values, set your goals and realistic expectations and you'll see how careful planning will ease your life.

Parental Leave and Flexible Work Arrangements

Many workplaces offer paternity leave, allowing fathers to take time off to bond with their newborns and support their partners during the postpartum period. Paternity leave policies vary by company and region, so familiarize yourself with your employer's offerings and rights under applicable laws. Taking advantage of paternity leave provides an invaluable opportunity to establish a strong foundation for your relationship with your child from the very beginning.

Negotiating Flexible Work Hours

Flexible work arrangements, such as telecommuting, flextime, or compressed workweeks, can provide fathers with greater autonomy over their schedules. Negotiate with your employer to explore options for adjusting your work hours or location to accommodate family commitments. Upon arrival of your new baby, flexibility at work will allow you to be present for doctor's appointments, or covering your partner so she could work and run errands or have mommy time for herself when needed.

Remote Work Opportunities

Thank You Covid! If the Covid Epidemic & shutdown provided us anything, it really pushed the advancements in technology, We all started more video conferencing, polished those fun backgrounds as remote work has become increasingly prevalent in many industries. If feasible, explore opportunities to work remotely, either on a full-time or part-time basis depending on your family financial needs. Remote work offers the flexibility to manage your workload from home or other locations, reducing commuting time and allowing for a better work-life balance. I must admit I have had many a meeting with the "Business Mullet" – Sports coat on top and shorts on bottom!

Shared Parental Leave

In some regions, shared parental leave policies allow parents to split the leave entitlement between both partners. This option provides greater flexibility for fathers to be actively involved in caregiving responsibilities during the early stages of their child's life. Explore whether shared parental leave is available in your jurisdiction and consider how it can support your family's needs.

Flexible Return-to-Work Plans

When returning to work after parental leave, discuss with your employer the possibility of implementing a phased or gradual return-to-work plan. This approach eases the transition back to full-time work, allowing you to gradually reintegrate into your professional role while still prioritizing your family commitments.

Utilizing Employer Resources

Take advantage of any resources or support programs offered by your employer to assist with work-life balance. This may include employee assistance programs, childcare assistance, or parental support groups. Understanding and leveraging these resources can help alleviate stress and facilitate a smoother integration of work and family life.

By exploring options for parental leave and flexible work arrangements, fathers can actively engage in caregiving responsibilities, strengthen their bond with their children, and maintain fulfilling careers. Prioritize open communication with your employer, advocate for supportive policies, and embrace opportunities that enable you to achieve a harmonious work-family balance.

Maintaining Professional Growth

Let's break down the essentials of maintaining professional growth while rocking the dad life. It's all about keeping that career train moving while still being the superhero your family needs.

1. **Continuous Learning and Skill Development:** Keep that brain of yours hungry for knowledge. Whether it's signing up for courses, attending workshops, or diving into online seminars, staying sharp in your field keeps you ahead of the game.
2. **Networking and Relationship Building:** It's not just about what you know, but who you know. Make connections, join professional groups, and mingle with folks in your industry. You never know when a networking opportunity might lead to your next big career move.

3. **Setting Career Goals:** Aim high, my friend! Set those SMART goals–specific, measurable, achievable, relevant, and time-bound. Having clear objectives gives you a roadmap to success and keeps you focused on the prize.

4. **Seeking Feedback and Mentorship:** Don't be afraid to ask for feedback. It's like having your cheerleading squad guiding you along the way. And don't sleep on mentorship–having someone wise in your corner can be a game-changer.

5. **Balancing Work and Family Commitments:** Work hard, play harder, but don't forget about family time. Set those boundaries and make sure to carve out quality moments with your loved ones. Flexible work arrangements are your best friend here.

6. **Embracing Adaptability and Resilience:** Roll with the punches, my friend. Life throws curveballs, but it's how you swing that bat that counts. Stay adaptable, stay resilient, and you'll come out on top every time.

So, keep these tips in your back pocket as you navigate the wild world of career and fatherhood, with a little strategy and a lot of heart. However, while rocking career and dadship is great, you still need to have boundaries.

Establishing boundaries is like drawing lines in the sand that define where work ends, and family life begins. It's about creating a balance between your professional responsibilities and your personal commitments. Here are some tips to help you set effective boundaries:

1. **Define your work hours:** Be clear about when your workday starts and ends. Communicate these hours to your employer, colleagues, and clients, and stick to them as

much as possible. This helps manage expectations and prevents work from encroaching on your personal time.

2. **Carve out a dedicated workspace:** Having a designated area in your home for work can signal to yourself and others that when you're in that space, you're focused on work. When you leave that space, mentally switch gears into family mode to fully engage with your loved ones. When working at the office, I always recommended in your planner to recap what you were able to accomplish, and schedule your agenda for your next day, then flush your mind from work as it just adds anxiety….. you are done for the day and ready for your family. Same is true as you are going to work, you need to flush all the family challenges and go in to work mode. If you ever scene the old Sylvester Stallone movie "Over The Top" when he turns his trucker hat around, his entire attitude changes and he is ready for business…. We all can have a little Stallone in us!

3. **Prioritize family time:** Make sure to set aside uninterrupted time for your family without any work distractions. Whether it's sharing meals, bedtime routines, or weekend adventures, give your loved ones your undivided attention during these moments. It's these moments they will remember when they are older.

4. **Communicate your boundaries:** Be upfront with your employer, colleagues, and family members about your boundaries. Let them know when you're available for work and when you need to focus on your family. By communicating your needs clearly, you can ensure that others respect your time and commitments.

Setting boundaries isn't about shutting people out; it's about creating a healthy balance that allows you to excel in both your professional and personal life. So, take charge of your time, communicate your needs, and create space for what matters most–your family.

Be realistic about what you can accomplish within a given timeframe and set realistic expectations for yourself and others. Learn to delegate tasks, prioritize projects that are crucial for your job performance, and say no to additional responsibilities when necessary to prevent yourself from being overwhelmed and burned out. Remember that it's okay to ask for help and seek support when needed.

Incorporate self-care practices into your daily routine to recharge and replenish your energy reserves. Whether it's exercise, meditation, hobbies, or spending time outdoors, choose those activities that promote your physical, mental, and emotional well-being. And most importantly, go with the ones you enjoy most. By taking care of yourself, you'll be better equipped to fulfill your responsibilities both at work and at home.

Remain flexible and adaptable in adjusting your boundaries as needed to accommodate changing circumstances. Be open to reevaluating and renegotiating your boundaries periodically to ensure they remain effective in supporting your overall well-being and work-life balance.

By setting clear boundaries and honoring them consistently, you can create a healthy and sustainable balance between your work and family life, fostering greater fulfillment, happiness, and harmony in both realms.

Communication with Employers

It's always important to discuss your family-related needs you might have with your employer. Collaborating with your boss to find solutions that accommodate both your family responsibilities and work obligations is important. Here's a breakdown of effective communication strategies for navigating this conversation:

1. **Initiating the Conversation:** Initiate the discussion by scheduling a meeting or finding an appropriate time to speak with your employer. Approach the conversation professionally, emphasizing your dedication to your role while also highlighting the importance of achieving a healthy work-life balance.

2. **Clearly Articulating Your Needs:** Communicate your specific family-related needs, such as flexible work hours or work from home options. Provide concrete examples of how these accommodations can benefit both you and the organization, such as increased productivity.

3. **Highlighting the Business Case:** Frame your requests within the context of the company's objectives and values. Demonstrate how accommodating your family needs aligns with the organization's goals and can contribute to its overall success.

4. **Offering Solutions:** Propose potential solutions or alternatives that address your family's needs while minimizing disruption to workflow or productivity. Be open to brainstorming ideas and collaborating with your employer to find mutually beneficial arrangements.

5. **Anticipating Concerns:** Anticipate any potential concerns or objections your employer may have and address them proactively. Offer reassurances or solutions to mitigate any perceived risks and demonstrate your commitment to finding a workable solution.

6. **Seeking Feedback and Clarification:** Encourage open dialogue and invite your employer to provide feedback and ask questions. Listen actively to their concerns and be

prepared to clarify any misunderstandings or provide
additional information as needed.

7. **Negotiating and Compromising:** Be willing to negotiate
   and compromise to find mutually acceptable solutions that
   meet both your needs and the organization's requirements.
   Consider alternative options that may better align with
   your employer's preferences while still addressing your
   core concerns.

8. **Documenting Agreements:** Once an agreement is
   reached, document the terms and conditions of any
   flexible work arrangements or accommodations in
   writing. Clarify expectations, responsibilities, and any
   relevant deadlines to ensure clarity and accountability for
   both parties.

By approaching the conversation with professionalism and clarity,
you can create a supportive and collaborative conversation with
your employer that enables you to effectively discuss your work
and family responsibilities. Be open and talk to your boss about
having some flexibility at work as a new dad that will allow you to
care for your family and meet your job obligations.

CULTIVATING A THRIVING FAMILY LIFE

Creating a kick-azz family life isn't rocket science–it's about
cherishing the small, everyday moments and cultivating strong
connections that withstand the test of time. It's not about grand
gestures or elaborate plans; instead, it's about finding joy in the
simple things and building meaningful bonds with your loved
ones.

One of the keys to creating a "perfect" family life is prioritizing
quality time together. In today's busy world, it's easy to get caught

up in work, school, and other obligations, but setting aside dedicated time to spend with your family is essential. Whether it's enjoying a meal together, playing a board game, or going for a walk in the park all without (dare I say) monitoring our phones constantly, these shared experiences help strengthen your family bond and create lasting memories.

Communication is another crucial aspect of building a wonderful family life. Encourage open and honest communication among family members, where everyone feels heard and valued. This includes not only discussing important topics but also sharing stories, dreams, and aspirations. There is also a huge difference between being heard and someone listening. Thee is also a big difference and lessons to be learned with our children to understand that even though we hear you, doesn't mean you get whaat you want…. This may come as a shock to them! By fostering a culture of communication within your family, you can deepen your connections and strengthen your relationships.

Flexibility is crucial for any family. Life is unpredictable, and things don't always go as planned. Instead of getting bogged down by setbacks or disappointments, embrace flexibility and adaptability. Find creative solutions to challenges and remember that it's okay to change course if necessary. By being flexible, you can navigate life's ups and downs together as a family with grace and resilience.

Finally, don't forget to prioritize self-care as part of your family routine. Taking care of yourself is essential for your well-being, and it sets a positive example for your family members. Engage your loved ones to join you for walks or hikes and make it a regular habit. Reading books or having other hobbies are also great options that will promote mental well-being and recharge everyone's batteries.

Dad's Downtime–Nurturing Your Self-Dadness!

So, you're up to your elbows in diaper changes, simultaneously trying to assist with a work assignment, and rushing to the rescue as the designated superhero to mend those perpetually broken toys or kill a spider for your partner. Amidst the whirlwind of parental responsibilities, it's incredibly easy to lose sight of your own identity and needs. That's where the tale of Cap, a father of five, comes into play. Cap is the epitome of a dad who has mastered the delicate art of balance amid the chaos.

Before Cap became a dad, he was all about chasing that six-pack, killing it at work, and basically, being a total rockstar(he actually was in a band). However, as each tiny addition to his family entered the picture, his priorities underwent a significant transformation. Gone were the days of solely focusing on personal pursuits; instead, Cap found himself navigating the intricate dance between work, family, and self-care.

Life threw Cap a curveball–a health scare that hit him like a ton of bricks. While at work, he experienced intense chest pains and shortness of breath, prompting a rush to the emergency room. After undergoing thorough medical examinations and tests, doctors discovered that Cap had developed high blood pressure and was at risk of a potential heart attack if he didn't prioritize his health. This sobering revelation propelled Cap into reevaluating his lifestyle choices and placing a renewed emphasis on self-care and spending quality time with his family.

Suddenly, he found himself facing the stark reality that his well-being and precious time with loved ones trumped any career aspirations. While he still harbored ambitions to excel in his professional endeavors, Cap's perspective underwent a profound shift. You can't provide for your family if your 6 feet under!

Fast forward to today, and Cap is on a mission to strike that elusive balance between being present for his kids and taking care of himself. Though the days of chasing after a six-pack may be a thing of the past (for now), he's committed to staying active, fueling his body with nourishing foods, and prioritizing his overall health. After all, his children depend on him now more than ever, and he's determined to be there for them every step of the way.

So, what's the key takeaway from Cap's journey? Firstly, prioritizing self-care isn't selfish—it's an essential component of effective parenting. Just as you ensure your kids are happy and healthy, it's imperative to extend the same level of care to yourself. Having a health scare shouldn't be the kick in the back side you need. Whether it's carving out time for a leisurely hike, perfecting your golf swing, or simply indulging in a good book, nurturing your own well-being sets a positive example for your children as well.

Furthermore, don't hesitate to set boundaries and reach out for support when needed. You don't have to navigate the challenges of parenthood alone, and leaning on your partner or family members can provide much-needed relief and assistance.

As you guessed, staying true to yourself is paramount. Whether you're passionate about sports, music, or DIY projects, don't let fatherhood overshadow your individual interests and passions. By prioritizing self-expression and pursuing activities that bring you joy, you'll not only maintain your sanity but also impart valuable lessons to your children about the importance of pursuing one's passions. Trust me, they are always watching!

So, embracing your inner "dadness" and prioritizing your own well-being are vital components of navigating the world of parenting. By investing in yourself, you'll cultivate the resilience and strength needed to show up fully for your family and be the amazing dad you were destined to be. And remember, finding that delicate balance is an ongoing journey—one that requires continual adjustments, but one that ultimately leads to a fulfilling and rewarding parenting experience. So, keep tweaking, keep adjusting, and above all, keep being the kick-ass dad that you are.

Up next: I sat down and talked to some seasoned dads and asked what advice they had for a new guy.

CHAPTER 8
DAD DIARIES

REFLECTING ON THE RIDICULOUS AND REMARKABLE IN THE NEVER-ENDING DADVENTURE

You know the old saying: "Time flies when you're having fun." Well, I think that is the reason our kids grow so fast because, believe me, in the blink of an eye, it's going to be their first birthday, then their second, and before you know it—they're off to school making friends, and start calling you old man.

That's why it's so important to soak in every moment of your adventure—the good, the messy, and the downright hilarious. Through sleepless nights and endless burps on your shoulder, you'll discover the true meaning of unconditional love. You'll learn that being a dad isn't just about providing for your little one—it's about being present, patient, and always ready for a game of peekaboo.

I know at this moment things might be scary, you might be feeling insecure, and don't know how the freak you're going to do this.

Take a deep breath and hear me out—you'll quickly master the art of multitasking like juggling work deadlines and soothe a fussy baby with one hand while flipping pancakes with the other.

Embrace the chaos, find joy in the everyday moments, and tackle the unpredictability of parenthood.

Amidst the chaos, you'll also discover the power of presence. Whether it's cuddling up for bedtime stories or chasing bubbles in the backyard, it's those simple moments spent together that create memories that last a lifetime.

As you look ahead to the next chapter of your dadventure, remember to savor the journey. Keep cherishing those silly giggles, messy milestones, and late-night cuddles. And don't forget to lean on your fellow dads for advice, support, and the occasional dad joke to lighten the mood.

LESSONS FROM DAD'S TO DAD'S

There's no substitute for the wisdom gained through firsthand experience, and seasoned fathers have a wealth of valuable insights to offer to those going through the journey of fatherhood. Learning from others can provide invaluable guidance, support, and perspective. It will also help newbies to cruise the challenges and joys of parenting with confidence and grace.

That is why I have enlisted the help and advice of other seasoned fathers who have weathered the ups and downs of being a parent. Dads who understand the importance of patience, resilience, and unconditional love. They've mastered raising their kids through trial and error, celebrating successes, and learning from mistakes along the way. Their advice is grounded in real-world experience, offering practical tips and strategies for navigating the complexities of bringing up kiddos. Jason Kelce, the legendary Philadelphia Eagles player and a proud father of three girls, in his retirement speech shared a profound sentiment about fatherhood, "I am a product of my upbringing. I think one of the best things a person can be in this world is a father. A father who is present, loving, and devoted just might be the greatest gift a child could ask for in this society." You don't have to be perfect; you just have to be present! Put in the effort, learn from mistakes you WILL make, and you'll be the best dad your kids could wish for.

Kelce's message serves as a reminder that perfection isn't necessary in fatherhood. Instead, it's about putting in the effort, learning from mistakes inevitably made along the way, and above all, loving unconditionally. Parenthood is a journey filled with unpredictability, but the impact of a father's presence and devotion is immeasurable.

So, be there for your children, cherish every moment, and strive to be the best father you can be. Remember, it's not about being flawless–it's about being there for them and showing unwavering love and support.

Let's dive in and see what other dads have to say:

Tony (father of two) on the Gift of Patience

Let me drop some truth on you: Patience isn't just a nice thing to have; it's your secret weapon for effective parenting. When you can keep your cool during chaos, you're setting the stage for a loving and nurturing environment for your little one.

You're gonna face some wild moments–from diaper blowouts to toddler meltdowns–it's all part of the adventure. But here's where patience comes in. When things get crazy, take a deep breath, count to ten if you need to, and respond with love and understanding.

Why does patience matter so much? Well, for starters, it builds trust between you and your kiddo. When they see that you're calm and collected, even when they're losing their mind over the wrong color cup (and, yes, that does happen more than you think), it shows them that you've got their back no matter what.

Plus, patience is like a superpower when it comes to teaching your kid important life skills. When you handle challenges with patience and grace, you're showing them how to problem-solve and deal with big feelings in a healthy way.

Now, here's the thing: Patience isn't always easy. There will be days when you're exhausted, stressed, and ready to throw in the towel. But trust me, my friend, those are the days when patience matters most.

So, here's my advice to you, newbie dad: Embrace the chaos, breathe through the tough moments, and remember that patience is your greatest ally on this wild ride called parenthood.

You've got this!

Alex's (father of three) Advice: Surround Yourself with Male Role Models

Let me clue you in on something crucial: Surround yourself with experienced fathers or mentors. It's like having a cheat code for parenthood. These guys have been around the block and can offer some seriously valuable advice and perspective.

Being a dad is not an easy enterprise. But having someone who's been there, done that, and survived to tell the tale can make all the difference. Whether it's your own dad, an uncle, a friend, or a neighbor, seek out those veterans who can share their wisdom with you.

Why is this important? Well, let me tell you. These guys have seen it all–the sleepless nights, the poo art on the walls, the epic tantrums–and they survived. They know the ins and outs of fatherhood like the back of their hand, so they've definitely got something to share.

Don't be afraid to reach out and ask for help. Whether you need advice on soothing a fussy baby or navigating the teenage years, these guys have got your back. Plus, having a support network of fellow dads can make the journey a whole lot less lonely and a whole lot more fun.

Trust me, surrounding yourself with male role models is one of the best things you can do for yourself and your family. So, go ahead, reach out, and soak up all the wisdom these guys have to offer, and typically it may cost you a beer or a cup of joe!

Dave (father of six) Says: Love Your Kids' Mom

Loving your kids' mom isn't just about romance; it's about building a solid, respectful relationship with the woman who's co-piloting this crazy journey of parenthood with you.

When you and your partner are on the same page and showing each other love and respect, it sets the tone for your whole family. Your kids pick up on that vibe, and it creates a safe, nurturing environment for them to grow and thrive.

So, how do you do this?

It's all about communication, compromise, and showing appreciation for each other. Take the time to listen to your partner, even when you're knee-deep in the routine of feedings, soothing, and playtime. And don't forget to express gratitude for all the little things they do to keep your family running smoothly.

But here's the thing: It's not always easy. Parenthood can be stressful, and there will be times when you butt heads with your partner. That's totally normal! The key is to approach those moments with love and understanding and to remember you're a team.

Why do you need to pay that much attention to this? Well, besides the obvious benefits for your relationship, it's also a powerful example for your kids. When they see Mom and Dad treat each other with kindness and respect, it sets the bar high for their own future relationships.

If you're not in a relationship with your kids' mom, that's okay, too. The important thing is still to cultivate a positive and respectful co-parenting relationship with her.

Even if you're not together romantically, you're still partners in raising your children. That means communicating openly and honestly, making decisions together, and showing each other respect and support. I have seen so many split families where one parent talks negatively about the other and it's just sad. What kind of message are you sending to that child. Should a child ever have to choose or hear someone they love talk bad about someone else they love?

Remember, your kids are watching how you interact with their mom, so it's crucial to keep things positive and amicable. Even if you don't always see eye to eye, try to focus on what's best for your children and find common ground where you can.

Co-parenting can be challenging, especially if there are unresolved issues from your past relationship, but working together can make a world of difference for your kids' well-being.

So, whether you're in a relationship with your kids' mom or not, the key is still to prioritize open communication, mutual respect, and cooperation for the sake of your children.

Peter (father of two) Advises: Take Care of Your Own Health

You have probably heard this before, but I want to emphasize it again—taking care of yourself is paramount. Yep, I'm talking about prioritizing your mental, physical, emotional, and spiritual well-being.

I view parenting as a marathon, not a sprint. And just like you wouldn't try to run a marathon without training and taking care of yourself, you can't be the best parent you can be if you're running on empty.

So, how do you do this?

It's all about carving out time for self-care and making it a priority. That means taking breaks when you need them, getting enough sleep (I know, it's hard sometimes but try your best!), eating healthy, and finding activities that recharge your batteries. It's not selfish to take care of yourself—it's essential. When you're feeling refreshed and energized, you're better equipped to handle the challenges of parenting with patience and a clear head.

Plus, by prioritizing your own well-being, you're setting a powerful example for your kids. You're showing them the importance of self-care and teaching them that it's essential to prioritize their own health, too.

So, whether it's going for a run, meditating, or just taking a few minutes to yourself with a cup of coffee, make sure to carve out some time for self-care. You—and your kids—will thank you for it.

Brent (daddy to four girls) on Being Present in Your Child's Life

Time flies when you're raising kids. Before you know it, they'll be all grown up and out the door. One moment your little one's laughter fills the room as you play together on the floor or when their tiny hand reaches up to hold yours as you walk hand in hand to the park, and you watch with pride as they take their first wobbly steps, and you share in their excitement as they discover the world around them.

These are the moments I'm talking about–the ones that make parenthood truly magical. However, life moves at lightning speed, and if we're not careful, we can miss out on these precious moments altogether.

That's why it's so important to be present and engaged in your child's life. It's not just about physically being there; it's about truly being in the moment, soaking up every second of their childhood.

When you're present, you're not just going through the motions, you're not checking messages on your phone or watching the TV in the background–you're fully invested in the experience. You're listening with your heart as well as your ears, and you're making memories that will last forever.

And here's the best part: Those moments of connection lay the foundation for strong parent-child relationships. When your child knows that you're there for them, that you're truly present and engaged in their lives, it creates a bond that can withstand anything life throws your way.

So, don't let those precious moments slip away. You most likely will not remember what you watched on TV on Thursday night, but you will remember when she first calls you DaDa! Cherish every hug, every laugh, every bedtime story. Because before you know it, they'll be all grown up, and you'll be left with nothing but memories.

Embrace every moment, Dad. You won't regret it!

Chris (father of five): Choose Quality Time with Your Child

There are so many things I can say but, for me, the best advice I can give is to spend quality time with your kiddo. I'm not just talking about being in the same room while they're glued to their tablet. I mean really connecting with them–heart to heart, soul to soul.

Meaningful interactions and shared experiences are the cement that holds a family together. When you spend quality time with your child, you're not just building memories; you're building a bond.

So, how to approach this best?

It's all about finding activities that you both enjoy and that allow you to connect on a deeper level. Whether it's playing a game, going for a hike, or just having a chat. Try to carve out time for these special moments as they bring you two closer together the more you interact. I have played basketball for hours with my oldest, and some of our conversations on that driveway, will be some of my fondest memories for sure.

Why does this matter so much?

Well, for starters, it fosters a sense of connection and belonging within the family unit. When your child knows that they're valued and loved, it creates a strong foundation for their emotional well-being.

Plus, quality time with your child is an investment in your relationship. It shows them that you care about them, and you are there for them when they need you.

So, to all the new dads reading this, don't underestimate the power of quality time with your kiddo. It's not just about filling the hours—it's about filling their heart with love, trust and understanding while creating memories that will last a lifetime.

Tom (Padre to two) Says: Know the Details of Your Kids' Lives

Being involved in your child's interests, activities, and daily experiences is like adding rocket fuel to your relationship. When you show up and take an interest in what matters to them, you're sending a powerful message: "I care about you, and I'm here to support you."

So, what does this look like in practice?

It's about asking questions, listening attentively, and showing genuine enthusiasm for whatever your child is into. Whether they're into sports, music, art, or something else, take the time to learn about it and get involved.

Why does this matter so much?

First of all, it shows your child that you're invested in their happiness and well-being. When they see that you're paying attention and taking an interest in their life, it boosts their confidence and strengthens the bond between you two.

Also, staying involved allows you to offer support, guidance, and encouragement when your child needs it most. Whether they're struggling with a tricky math problem or dealing with friendship drama at school, knowing that you're there to help can make all the difference in the world.

In sum, what I'm trying to say is don't be a bystander in your child's life—be an active participant. Show up, get involved, and watch your relationship grow stronger day after day.

Martin (dad to Martin IV): Give Physical & Verbal Affection

I would advise that it's absolutely crucial in parenting to give physical and verbal affection to your kids. This isn't just about showing them that you care–it's about creating a warm and loving environment where they can thrive.

Kids need love like plants need sunlight. It's essential for their emotional and psychological development and this starts immediately when you hold them in the delivery room. So, don't hold back on the hugs, kisses, and kind words. Shower them with affection every chance you get.

Why is this so important?

Because physical affection releases feel-good hormones like oxytocin, which helps your child feel safe, secure, and loved. It also strengthens your bond with them and fosters a sense of closeness and connection.

But it's not just about the physical stuff. Verbal affection is just as important. Telling your kids that you love them, that you're proud of them, and that you believe in them can do wonders for their self-esteem and confidence.

Don't be shy about expressing your love and appreciation to your kids. Whether it's a big bear hug, a kiss on the forehead, or simply saying "I love you." These small gestures can make a world of difference in your child's life.

Travis (father of seven): Model Healthy Financial Habits

I suppose my advice might not be the most glamorous, but I think it's super important. Teaching your kids about money. Yep, it's never too early to start instilling good financial habits in your little ones.

By showing them the ropes when it comes to spending, saving, and budgeting, you're setting them up for success later in life. Trust me, they'll thank you for it!

So, how do you do this?

It's all about leading by example. Let your kids see you making smart financial choices, like sticking to a budget, saving for big purchases, and avoiding unnecessary splurges.

But it's not just about what you do–it's also about what you say. Take the time to explain the reasoning behind your financial decisions and involve your kids in the process. Let them help you create a budget, save up for a family vacation, or decide how to spend their allowance.

Teaching your kids about money empowers them to take control of their financial future. It gives them the tools they need to make smart choices and avoid falling into common money traps. I know it's not their favorite gift on their birthday, but I give them bonds and discuss what those will be worth to them down the road.

Plus, by instilling good financial habits early on, you're setting them up for success in the long run. Whether it's saving up for college, buying their first car, or investing for retirement, they'll have the skills and knowledge they need to navigate the world of finance with confidence. Don't underestimate the power of teaching your children about money. It's one of the most valuable lessons you can pass on to them, and it will pay dividends for years to come.

Derek (dad of two) Says: Eat Together as a Family

This might sound petty simple, but it packs a powerful punch– eating together as a family. Maybe this is due to my big Italian family and my memories as a child, but I still believe it's true today.

You know gathering around the table for meals isn't just about satisfying hunger—it's about building bonds and creating memories.

Family meals are like the glue that holds a family together. When you make mealtime a priority, you're sending a message that says, "We're in this together, and we value spending time with each other."

It's all about carving out time in your busy schedule to sit down and enjoy a meal together. Whether it's breakfast, lunch, or dinner, try to make it a regular occurrence and a time when everyone can come to the table to break bread.

But it's not just about the food(or Wine)—it's also about the conversation. Use mealtime as an opportunity to catch up on each other's day, share stories, and laugh together. Put away the phones and other distractions and focus on being present.

Having meals together fosters a sense of unity within the family. When all the family members sit down at the table(and if your Italian-that's a lot of family), you're creating a shared experience that strengthens your bonds and reinforces your sense of belonging.

Plus, research shows that families who eat together have stronger relationships and healthier eating habits. So, by making mealtime a priority, you're not just nourishing your bodies—you're also nourishing your souls.

The main point is don't underestimate the power of eating together as a family. It's a simple yet powerful way to strengthen your familial bonds and create lasting memories with the ones you love.

More Tips and Tricks of Parenting

The following tips and tricks are from other dads who think the things listed below are important when raising children. Here is what they say:

Involving Your Kids in Creating Rules and Discipline

When you involve your kids in creating rules and discipline, it isn't just about laying down the law–it's about empowering your kids to be active participants in shaping their behavior and learning valuable life lessons on a daily basis.

When you bring your kids into the decision-making process around rules and discipline, you're giving them a voice and a stake in the outcome. It not only helps them understand the importance of boundaries and consequences but also fosters a sense of responsibility and accountability.

It's all about having open and honest conversations with your kids about why certain rules are in place and what the consequences will be if they're broken. Give them a chance to share their thoughts and feelings and work together to come up with solutions that everyone can agree on.

Communication teaches your kids that their actions have consequences and that they have the power to make positive choices. It also strengthens the parent-child bond and creates a sense of trust and mutual respect.

And the bonus of this is their successful lives in the long run. When involving your kids in creating rules and discipline, they'll learn valuable problem-solving skills, increase emotional intelligence, and strengthen self-discipline–all of which are essential for navigating the challenges of adulthood.

Don't be afraid to let your kids have a say in the rules. By working together as a team, you'll not only create a happier and more harmonious home environment but also raise responsible and independent individuals who are ready to take on the world.

Cultivating a Love for Reading and Learning

Cultivate a love for reading and learning in your kids from an early age. Trust me, it's one of the best gifts you can give them!

When you start early with reading and learning, you're laying the groundwork for academic success and a lifelong love of discovery. But it's not just about boosting their literacy skills–it's also about creating cherished memories and strengthening your bond as parent and child.

Make reading a part of your daily routine. Whether it's bedtime stories, trips to the library, or cozy reading sessions on the couch, allocate some time to share stories and books with your kids.

As we all know, reading opens a world of imagination and possibility for your kids. It helps them develop language skills, expand their vocabulary, and sharpen their critical thinking abilities. And it's a great way to bond with your kids and create lasting memories together.

However, it's not just about the educational benefits. Reading also fosters empathy, compassion, and a deeper understanding of the world around us. By exposing your kids to a diverse range of stories and perspectives, you're helping them become more compassionate and open-minded individuals. It's a simple yet powerful way to ignite their curiosity, expand their horizons, and strengthen their relationships with you.

Avoid Overparenting

Let's talk about a crucial aspect of parenting–avoiding overparenting. It's natural to want to protect your kids from harm and guide them every step of the way, but sometimes, less is more.

Giving your kids the space to explore, take risks, and learn from their mistakes is essential for their growth and development. Overparenting, on the other hand, can stifle their independence and resilience.

Offer them guidance and support when needed but also allow your kids the freedom to learn and grow on their own. Let them make mistakes, let them fail, and let them figure things out for themselves.

Why does this matter so much?

It builds resilience. When your kids face challenges and setbacks on their own, they learn valuable lessons about perseverance and problem-solving. And it boosts their self-confidence and sense of independence.

There is more in this. When you give your kids the freedom to explore and make their own choices, you also help them to promote creativity, curiosity, and a sense of ownership over their lives.

So, resist the urge to hover over your kids every minute of the day (Okay, you can do that just a little bit). Trust that you've equipped them with the skills and knowledge they need to navigate the world on their own and give them the space to spread their wings and fly.

By embracing these lessons from seasoned dads and staying committed to continual growth of your kiddo and your relationships with them, you'll navigate the joys and challenges of fatherhood with confidence, grace, and a deep sense of fulfillment.

As you look back on the early days of parenting and gaze forward to the unknown path ahead, you realize that this journey is far more than a series of milestones and destinations—it's about nurturing the ever-expanding heart of a father. Each day brings new experiences, challenges, and joys, shaping you into the parent you're meant to be.

With every sunrise, your role evolves, unveiling fresh layers of happiness and presenting hurdles to conquer. Yet, through it all, your love remains steadfast and unwavering. It's a love that knows no bounds, fueled by patience, dedication, and an unyielding commitment to your child's well-being.

As you navigate the twists and turns of parenthood, remember that your influence extends far beyond the present moment. You're sculpting the future, leaving behind a legacy of love that will resonate for generations to come. Embrace each step of the journey, treasure the precious moments, and revel in the boundless capacity of a father's heart.

In the next, final, and bonus chapter, you'll find *50 Dad Hacks* to help you make your transition from an awesome guy to an awesome dad.

CHAPTER 9
BONUS: DAD HACKS
OVER 50 BONUS HACKS TO MAKE LIFE A LITTLE MORE SIMPLE

Welcome to the bonus chapter! Here, we dive deep into the exhilarating adventure of parenthood and uncover a treasure trove of invaluable tips and tricks to help you navigate the wild ride with finesse. From ensuring your child's safety to preserving your own sanity, this chapter is packed with practical advice and ingenious hacks that will not only make the journey of parenthood smoother but also amplify the joy and fulfillment along the way. Prepare to discover a wealth of insights that will empower you to tackle the challenges of parenting head-on while savoring every precious moment of the journey. With these expert strategies at your fingertips, you'll be equipped to navigate the twists and turns of parenthood with confidence and grace, creating cherished memories that will last forever. Will everyone of these work for you? Probably not, but if 1 or 5 do then you owe me an awesome review at the end of this. LoL

1. **Wear Your Baby:** It's a win-win situation. You can multitask while bonding with your little one. Besides, the gentle motion often helps to soothe them.

2. **No Honey Before One:** This is a crucial safety tip many parents overlook. Honey can harbor harmful bacteria in infants under one year old, so it's best to avoid it until they're older.

3. **Engagement Over Toys:** While toys can be fun, it's your interaction and engagement that truly stimulate your baby's development. So, save your money and focus on quality time together.

4. **Skip the Baby Walkers:** Not only can they be dangerous, but they also hinder a child's natural development of walking skills.

5. **Beware the Baby Boy Firehose (Remember Jay's story):** A quick wipe or some air circulation can prevent unexpected messes during diaper changes.

6. **Outsmart the Grabby Baby:** Use a gentle technique to release their grip during bath time, making your life a little easier. A gentle technique could be something like distracting them with a toy or softly blowing warm air on their fingers.

7. **Homemade Haircut Cape:** A simple trash bag can save you from a hairy situation during at-home haircuts.

8. **Sunblock While Strapped in:** Make sunblock application a breeze by doing it while your child is safely buckled up.

9. **Nail Clipping Secret:** Clip those tiny nails while they're snoozing to avoid any accidental nips.

10. **Inside-Out Shirt Hack:** Keep your clothes clean and snuggle-ready by wearing them inside out while at home.

11. **Shake Up Healthy Snacks:** Sneak some veggies into a tasty shake for a Hulk-worthy treat.

12. **Bilingual Books Boost Brainpower:** Start early with bilingual books to help your child's language development.

13. **Tax Everything with Kisses:** A sweet way to teach your toddler the concept of exchange and affection.

14. **Swaddle Solution:** When in doubt, use a pair of pants for impromptu swaddling until you find the proper gear.

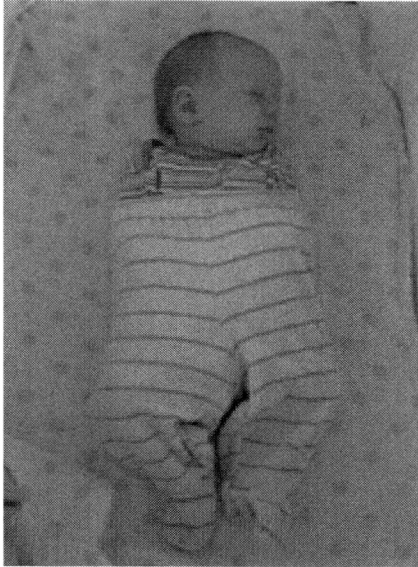

15. Bootcamp for dads had this great idea to allow kids to be creative, yet not on your walls of furniture:

16. **Fennel Seeds for Gas Relief:** A teaspoon of fennel seeds can work wonders for easing gas pains in both kids and adults. Just have them chew on some seeds, and that discomfort will disappear in no time.

17. **No Toys in Bed for Light Sleepers:** Keeping toys out of bed helps prevent distractions and encourages better sleep habits for your little one. Save the playtime for when it's not sleepy time.

18. **Washable Art Supplies**: Save your walls from artistic masterpieces by ensuring that all pens, markers, and crayons are washable. Cleanup will be a breeze when creativity strikes.

19. **Emergency Supplies in the Trunk:** Be prepared for any parenting emergency by keeping water, handwashing supplies, wet wipes, soap, and extra diapers and outfits in your trunk. Trust me, you'll thank yourself later.

20. **Cheerio Necklace:** Keep your toddlers entertained during long car rides or flights with a simple Cheerio necklace. It's a tasty snack and a fun activity rolled into one.

21. **Baby Food Maker:** Invest in a baby food maker to save time and money while ensuring your little one gets nutritious homemade meals. It's a win-win for both you and your baby's health.

22. **Ultimate Stain Remover:** Dawn Dish soap, Hydrogen Peroxide, and Baking Soda make a powerful stain-fighting trio. Say goodbye to stubborn stains on clothes, couches, or carpets.

23. **Organized Folding:** Simplify your life by folding pajamas or outfits together and rolling them up before storing them in drawers. It saves space and makes getting dressed a breeze.

24. **Gripe Water Pacifier Dip:** Calm your baby down by dipping their pacifier in Gripe Water instead of the old-fashioned bourbon method. It's a safer and more acceptable option.

25. **Tissue Trick for Sleep:** Stroke a tissue gently over your baby's face to help them settle down and fall asleep. It may sound unusual, but many parents swear by this technique.

26. **Layered Crib Sheets:** Save yourself from midnight sheet changes by layering crib sheets and mattress protectors. When accidents happen, simply strip off the top layer and reveal a fresh set underneath.

27. **To-Go Sauce Containers for Pacifiers:** Keep pacifiers clean on the go by storing them in small to-go sauce containers. They're perfect for tossing in your bag and keeping pacifiers germ-free.

28. **Medicine Dropper Pacifier Trick:** Administer medicine to your baby by sticking a dropper through an already-cut pacifier. It's a clever way to make medicine time a little easier.

29. **Adhesive Hook for Bibs:** Keep bibs handy during mealtime by sticking an adhesive hook on the back of your highchair. It's a simple solution for keeping messes at bay.

30. **Cable Ties for Baby Gates:** Secure baby gates without damaging your banister by using cable ties. They provide a sturdy hold and can be easily removed when the gate is no longer needed.

31. **Fake Video Game Remotes:** Keep your kids entertained while you play video games by giving them fake remote controls. They'll feel included without interrupting your gaming session.

32. **Rice Glove Trick:** Mimic your touch and help your baby drift off to sleep by warming a glove filled with rice in the microwave and placing it next to them in the crib.

33. **Multiple Diaper Changing Stations:** Save time and

effort by creating several diaper-changing stations around your home. Having all the essentials in reach can be a lifesaver during diaper emergencies.

34. **Diaper Box Storage:** Utilize diaper boxes for storing outgrown clothes or baby items you're not currently using. They're sturdy and can help keep things organized.

35. **Mesh Laundry Bag for Baby Socks:** Keep baby socks together during washing and drying by using a mesh laundry bag. Say goodbye to lost socks!

36. **Fitted Sheet for Car Seat:** Prevent stains in your car by placing a fitted sheet under your baby's car seat. It can catch spills and crumbs, making cleanup as easy as possible.

37. **Extra Shirt for Yourself While Traveling:** Always pack an extra shirt for yourself when traveling with a baby. You never know when spit-ups or blowouts might happen!

38. **Remove Onesies from Shoulders Down During Pooptastrophes:** When dealing with a pooptastrophe, always remove the onesie from the shoulders down to minimize mess and avoid spreading it further. We all just got the mental image!

39. **Double Bag Dirty Diapers:** Trap odors by double bagging dirty diapers before disposing of them in your diaper genie. Your nose will thank you for this trick!

40. **Bounce on Exercise Ball to Calm Newborns:** Soothe a fussy newborn by bouncing on a big exercise ball. The gentle motion can work wonders in calming them down.

41. **Frozen Binky for Teething Relief:** Fill a binky with water and freeze it for instant teething relief. It soothes sore gums and provides comfort to your little one.

42. **Marshmallows as Cold Packs:** Use frozen marshmallows in a freezer bag to soothe bumps and bruises. They offer a soft and gentle alternative to traditional cold packs.

43. **Training Potty for Travel:** Keep a training potty with a diaper in it for locations without a bathroom or for road trips. It's a convenient solution for potty training on the go.

44. **Utilize Naptime Wisely:** Use naptime efficiently by avoiding tasks that can be done while your baby is awake. Take the opportunity to rest and recharge yourself.

45. **Multi-Tasking in the Bathroom:** Save time by brushing your teeth while using the bathroom. It's a practical way to make the most of your limited time as a parent.

46. **Diaper Distraction Trick:** Keep your baby distracted during diaper changes by placing a wipe on their forehead. It keeps them occupied long enough for you to change their diaper without any fuss.

47. **Avoid Eye Contact at Night:** When attending to your baby's needs at night, avoid making eye contact to prevent them from thinking it's playtime. Comfort them with hugs and kisses but maintain a calm and soothing environment.

48. **Swing the Car Seat for Soothing:** Once your baby is securely strapped in the car seat, gently swing it like a pendulum to calm them down. It's a simple yet effective way to soothe a crying baby.

49. **Protective Mitts for Scratching:** Prevent scratches from your baby's sharp nails by putting scratch mitts or socks on their hands while they sleep. It keeps their little hands protected and prevents any accidental scratches.

50. **Accept Imperfection and Love:** Understand that you won't always get everything right, and that's okay. Care for your child and be present for them every time you can–this is the most important "dad hack" you need. Embrace the journey of fatherhood with love and patience. You're doing great!

With these clever parenting hacks, you'll be better equipped to tackle the challenges of parenthood with ease and efficiency!

CONCLUSION

Alright, let's sum this up! So, being a dad? It's this crazy ride, packed with moments that'll make your heart soar, challenges that'll make you sweat, and chances for personal growth around every corner.

Now, getting into this whole dad gig starts with building a solid foundation. Think of it like a big ol' Lego tower, with positive role models, a strong bond with your kid's mom (or whoever's on mom duty), and support from loved ones. You also need to make sure you're taking care of yourself, too. Because, let's face it, you can't pour from an empty cup, right? It's all about being there. Like, really being present for your little one. Those tiny interactions, from tickle fights to bedtime stories, build that special bond between you and your kiddo.

And, hey, don't sweat it if you don't have all the answers right away. We're all just figuring this dad thing out as we go along. So, keep learning, stay in the loop, and don't be afraid to lean on your fellow dads for advice and support.

So, to sum it all up, being a great dad is about being there, being present, and being open to learning and soaking up on every opportunity the life throws at you. And, trust me, the journey? It's wild, it's messy, but man, is it so worth it.

Alright, let's break it down. Fatherhood is not a solo gig—you've already learned about it. It's like being part of this big, awesome team. And just like any team, you gotta have your buddies to lean on. Seeking advice, swapping stories, and sharing laughs with other dads is important for your mental health. That's where the magic happens. It's like having your own personal support squad, ready to cheer you on through the crazy ride of parenthood.

As your kiddo grows up, your parenting game's gotta evolve, too. Anticipating the curveballs life throws your way and rolling with the punches? That's the name of the game. By staying flexible and open to change, you're better equipped to handle whatever comes your way and adapt to your child's ever-changing needs. It's all about keeping that bond strong and the love flowing.

Now, let's talk about your dad game plan. Having a clear set of values and goals is your parenting playbook. It helps you make decisions and steer your child in the right direction. So, take some time to figure out what matters most to you and your family, and use that as your compass as you navigate this wild journey of fatherhood.

Finding that sweet spot between being a dad and pursuing your own dreams can be like juggling knives and bowling balls at once. However, trust me, it's worth it. When you show your kids that it's important to chase after what makes you happy, you're setting them up for success. So, whether it's mastering the grill or finally picking up that guitar, don't forget to make time for yourself.

Don't forget to soak up those magical moments with your little ones. From bedtime stories to belly laughs, these are the memories that'll stick with you forever. So, don't blink–you might just miss 'em! Being a dad is all about embracing the joy and love that comes with it. Every single day.

I like to share one last story about another awesome dad, Mark. Now, Mark was about as clueless as a goldfish in a maze when it came to babies. He could change a tire blindfolded and whip up a mean batch of chili, but when it came to swaddling and soothing a crying baby, he was as lost as a sock in the laundry.

One fateful morning, Mark was left alone with his precious bundle of joy while his partner, Sarah, dashed out to conquer the wilds of the grocery store. Little did he know that this mission impossible he was left in would be the ultimate test of his dad skills.

As soon as Sarah's car disappeared around the corner, chaos ensued. Baby Max unleashed a symphony of wails that echoed through the house like a herd of angry elephants. Mark panicked, frantically bouncing, and shushing the baby, but to no avail. It seemed that baby Max had declared war on sleep, and he was very upset.

In a desperate attempt to silence the cacophony of cries, Mark resorted to the ancient art of baby-wearing. Armed with a carrier that resembled a cross between a straitjacket and a backpack, he strapped baby Max to his chest and set off on a mission to lull him into dreamland.

But alas, baby Max had other plans. As Mark paced the living room, bouncing and swaying like a deranged marionette, he failed to notice the telltale signs of impending disaster. Suddenly, like a volcano erupting, baby Max unleashed a torrent of projectile vomit that painted the walls in shades of regurgitated formula. You will soon realize; there is no smell that compares to this.

In a panic, Mark rushed to the nursery, only to find that every spare onesie had been claimed by the laundry gods. With no other option, he grabbed the closest article of clothing—a Hawaiian shirt that hadn't seen the light of day since his ill-fated attempt at a luau-themed party—and fashioned it into a makeshift diaper.

Just as Mark was about to surrender to defeat, Sarah returned, armed with groceries and a look of horror at the scene before her. But instead of scolding Mark for his misadventures, she burst into laughter, tears streaming down her cheeks as she surveyed the chaos.

And so, amidst the chaos and calamity of first-time fatherhood, Mark learned an invaluable lesson: sometimes, you just have to roll with the punches, embrace the messiness of parenthood, and remember to laugh in the face of disaster. After all, isn't that what being a dad is all about?

With all the wisdom you've picked up along the way, it's time to dive into fatherhood headfirst. Your kiddo's counting on you to be their rock, their biggest cheerleader, and their guiding light. So, go ahead—show 'em what you're made of!

And, hey, if this book has been a game-changer for you, why not spread the love? Leave a review on Amazon and help other dads on their journey, too. After you have read this, and you feel it's been valuable and insightful, keep ahold of it till you have a friend or other dad that may need this. Inside the cover page, write down your advice on what you learned these first few years, and pass it along. After all, we're all in this together.

KEEPING THE GAME ALIVE

Congratulations on reaching the end of "Dads-to-Be: First-Time Fathers Guide"! By now, you've learned a ton of great strategies to balance being a super dad with everything else in your life. But the journey doesn't stop here.

It's time to pass on your newfound knowledge and show other soon-to-be dads where they can find the same help. Think back to when you first held this book in your hands, maybe feeling a mix of excitement and nerves about becoming a father. There are lots of other men out there right now feeling just like that, wondering if they can do it.

Here's where you can make a big difference with just a small action. Can you take a moment to share what you've learned by leaving a review? Your words could be the guiding light for another dad out there looking for support.

Leaving a review is easy and quick, and here's how you can do it:

Just scan the QR code below to share your thoughts:

Your experience could help another dad to:

- Feel more confident as he steps into fatherhood.

- Strengthen his relationship with his partner and children.

- Find the perfect balance between work and family life.

- Enjoy the journey of fatherhood with less stress and more joy.

Remember, every big journey starts with small steps. Your review is one small step for you, but a giant leap in helping other dads navigate this amazing path.

Thank you for trusting this guide to help you through your first steps into fatherhood. Now, let's keep the game alive by helping others play it well, too.

- Your friend and fellow dad, D. MoSon

P.S. - Sharing is caring! If you know another dad-to-be who could use some guidance, why not pass this book along? Write a few suggestions from your experience as a first-time dad in the cover along with some encouragement. It's a great way to keep the spirit of support and community going strong among fathers everywhere!

REFERENCES

Allen, L., & Kelly, B. B. (2019). *Child Development and Early Learning*. Nih.gov; National Academies Press (US). https://www.ncbi.nlm.nih.gov/books/NBK310550/

Breastfeeding. (2019, November 11). World Health Organization. https://www.who.int/health-topics/breastfeeding#tab=tab_1

De Sousa Machado, T., Chur-Hansen, A., & Due, C. (2020). First-time mothers' perceptions of social support: Recommendations for best practice. *Health Psychology Open*, *7*(1), 205510291989861. https://doi.org/10.1177/2055102919898611

Engqvist, I., & Nilsson, K. (2011). Men's experience of their partners' postpartum psychiatric disorders: narratives from the internet. *Mental Health in Family Medicine*, *8*(3), 137–146. https://www.ncbi.nlm.nih.gov/pmc/articles/PMC3314270/

4 strategies to be a better father. (2023). [YouTube Video]. Order of Man. https://www.youtube.com/watch?v=g7Gr-FCacXY&t=900s

Hey Shayla. (2022). *Minimalist: 5 baby essentials 1st 6 months* [YouTube Video]. https://www.youtube.com/watch?v=qWytjoaGNIE

Infant car seat installation. (2017). [YouTube Video]. BabyCenter. https://www.youtube.com/watch?v=FXZhHYcZpqg

Karp, Dr. H. (n.d.). *The 5 S's for Soothing Babies*. Happiest Baby. https://www.happiestbaby.com/blogs/baby/the-5-s-s-for-soothing-babies

Newborn Reflexes. (2019). Stanfordchildrens.org. https://www.stanfordchildrens.org/en/topic/default?id=newborn-reflexes-90-P02630

Pediatrician's top tips for newborn sleep. (2021). [YouTube Video]. The Doctors Bjorkman. https://www.youtube.com/watch?v=W44ohGqaicw

Pregnancy's Emotional Roller Coaster. (2000, August 28). WebMD. https://www.webmd.com/baby/features/pregnancy-emotional-roller-coaster

Pregnancy tips for dads–advice for expecting fathers. (2020). [YouTube Video]. Dad University. https://www.youtube.com/watch?v=aNK6UN7bXec

Prenatal vitamins: Why they matter, how to choose. (2018). Mayo Clinic. https://www.mayoclinic.org/healthy-lifestyle/pregnancy-week-by-week/in-depth/prenatal-vitamins/art-20046945

Singh, G., & Archana, G. (2008). Unraveling the mystery of vernix caseosa. *Indian Journal of Dermatology*, *53*(2), 54. https://doi.org/10.4103/0019-5154.41645

Teyler, B. (2020). *Practical baby products you ACTUALLY need | Baby registry must-haves* [YouTube Video]. https://www.youtube.com/watch?v=P4IMB2LB_jE

The Holy Bible: New International Version. (2011). *Proverbs 22:6*. Bible Study Tools. https://www.biblestudytools.com/proverbs/22-6.html

The Importance of Childbirth Education: 6 Reasons You Should Take Prenatal Classes | Roots Birth Center. (2022, December 5). Roots Community Birth Center. https://www.rootsbirthcenter.com/stories/2022/12/5/the-importance-of-childbirth-education-6-reasons-you-should-take-prenatal-classes

Tierney, A. L., & Nelson, C. A. (2009). Brain Development and the Role of Experience in the Early Years. *Zero to Three, 30*(2), 9–13. https://www.ncbi.nlm.nih.gov/pmc/articles/PMC3722610/

Yogman, M., Garner, A., Hutchinson, J., Hirsh-Pasek, K., & Golinkoff, R. M. (2018). The power of play: A pediatric role in enhancing development in young children. *Pediatrics, 142*(3). https://doi.org/10.1542/peds.2018-2058

Printed in Great Britain
by Amazon

50100364R00084